# RADICAL ORTHODOXY? – A CATHOLIC ENQUIRY

# HEYTHROP STUDIES
## IN CONTEMPORARY PHILOSOPHY, RELIGION & THEOLOGY

### Series Editor
Laurence Paul Hemming, Heythrop College, University of London, UK

### Series Editorial Advisory Board
John McDade SJ; Peter Vardy; Michael Barnes SJ; James Hanvey SJ;
Philip Endean SJ; Anne Murphy SHCJ

Drawing on renewed willingness amongst theologians and philosophers to enter into critical dialogues with contemporary issues, this series is characterised by Heythrop's reputation for openness and accessibility in academic engagement. Presenting volumes from a wide international, ecumenical, and disciplinary range of authors, the series explores areas of current theological, philosophical, historical, and political interest. The series incorporates a range of titles: accessible texts, cutting-edge research monographs, and edited collections of essays. Appealing to a wide academic and intellectual community interested in philosophical, religious and theological issues, research and debate, the books in this series will also appeal to a theological readership which includes enquiring lay-people, Clergy, members of religious communities, training priests, and anyone engaging broadly in the Catholic tradition and with its many dialogue partners.

# Radical Orthodoxy?
# – A Catholic Enquiry

*Edited by*
LAURENCE PAUL HEMMING

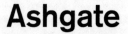

**Ashgate**

Aldershot • Burlington USA • Singapore • Sydney

Published by
Ashgate Publishing Ltd
Gower House
Croft Road
Aldershot
Hants GU11 3HR
England

Ashgate Publishing Company
131 Main Street
Burlington
Vermont 05401
USA

Ashgate website: http://www.ashgate.com

**British Library Cataloguing in Publication Data**
Radical orthodoxy? - a Catholic enquiry. - (Heythrop
     studies in contemporary philosophy, religion and theology)
     1. Catholic Church 2. Philosophical theology
     I. Hemming, Laurence Paul II. Heythrop College
     230'.046

**Library of Congress Control Number:** 00-29312

ISBN 0 7546 1292 9 (Hbk)
ISBN 0 7546 1293 7 (Pbk)

Printed and bound in Great Britain by MPG Books Ltd, Bodmin, Cornwall

# Contents

# List of Contributors

*David Burrell* CSC is Theodore Hesburgh Professor in Philosophy and Theology at the University of Notre Dame, Indiana, and has been working since 1982 in comparative issues in philosophical theology in Judaism, Christianity, and Islam. His many publications include *Knowing the Unknowable God: Ibn-Sina, Maimonides, Aquinas* (Indiana, Notre Dame University Press, 1986) and *Freedom and Creation in Three Traditions* (Indiana, Notre Dame University Press, 1993), as well as translations of al-Ghazali. He is currently directing the University of Notre Dame's Jerusalem program at the Tantur Ecumenical Institute.

*Oliver Davies* is Reader in Philosophical Theology at the University of Wales, Lampeter. He has written extensively on Mediæval mystical texts, including *Meister Eckhart Mystical Theologian* (London, SPCK, 1991) as well as translations of texts of the Rhineland mystics and the work of Hans Urs von Balthasar.

*Lucy Gardner* is Tutor in Christian Doctrine at St Stephen's House, Oxford. She is a co-author of *Balthasar at the End of Modernity* (Edinburgh, T&T Clark, 1999).

*James Hanvey* SJ is Head of Systematic Theology at Heythrop College, University of London. He is a member of the Editorial Advisory Board of *Heythrop Studies in Contemporary Philosophy, Religion and Theology*.

*Laurence Paul Hemming* is a Lecturer in the Systematic Theology Department at Heythrop College, University of London. He is an editor of the series *Heythrop Studies in Contemporary Philosophy, Religion, and Theology*.

*Fergus Kerr* OP is Regent of Blackfriars, Oxford, and Honorary Fellow of the Divinity Faculty at the University of Edinburgh. His publications include *Theology after Wittgenstein* (London, SPCK, 1997 [Oxford, Blackwell, 1986]) and *Immortal Longings: Versions of Transcending Humanity* (Indiana, University of Notre Dame Press, 1997). He is editor of *New Blackfriars*.

*John Milbank* is Francis Myers Ball Professor of Philosophical Theology at the University of Virginia, having previously held posts at Lancaster University and the University of Cambridge. He is the author of *The Religious Dimension in the Thought of Giambattista Vico* (Lampeter, Lewiston, 1991); *Theology and Social Theory: Beyond Secular Reason* (Oxford, Blackwell, 1990); and *The Word Made Strange: Theology, Language, Culture* (Oxford, Blackwell, 1997). He is also co-editor of *Radical Orthodoxy*.

*Catherine Pickstock* is a British Academy Post-doctoral Fellow at the Faculty of Divinity, University of Cambridge. She is author of *After Writing: On the Liturgical Consummation of Philosophy* (Oxford, Blackwell, 1998).

*Graham Ward* is Professor of Contextual Theology and Ethics at the University of Manchester. He is author of *Barth, Derrida, and the Language of Theology* (Cambridge, Cambridge University Press, 1995) and *Theology and Critical Theory* (London, Macmillan, 1996), as well as editor of *The Postmodern God* (Oxford, Blackwell, 1997) and *The de Certeau Reader* (Oxford, Blackwell, 1999).

# Acknowledgements

This book is the fruit of a conference held under the same title as this book, at Heythrop College in June 1999. I am grateful to all the speakers for making their papers available for publication. I would like to thank John McDade SJ and Peter Vardy for their advice and encouragement in establishing this new series.

I am grateful to Canon Herbert Veal, Parish Priest of the Catholic Church of Our Lady and the Holy Name of Jesus, Bow Common, London, for his permission to reproduce the jacket illustration.

I must also thank Fergus Kerr OP, Editor of *New Blackfriars* and a contributor to this volume, for his permission to reproduce parts of Catherine Pickstock's 1999 Oxford Aquinas Lecture here.

Finally, I owe a duty of thanks to Tony Hemming and Ferdinand Knapp for their patient advice and help with proofs.

*Solemnity of the Epiphany of the Lord*, 6th January, 2000.

# PART I
# INTRODUCTION

Chapter One

# Introduction
# Radical Orthodoxy's Appeal to Catholic Scholarship

Laurence Paul Hemming

The debate between Catholic theologians and Radical Orthodoxy[1] began in November 1997,when nearly fifty graduate students and faculty staff crammed into a room in the Divinity Faculty Building in Cambridge for the fortnightly seminar in philosophical theology. The excitement was tangible: students from other faculties sneaked in, fearful of ejection. Nicholas Lash, Norris Hulse Professor (now emeritus) was to deliver a paper on the work of John Milbank, himself then a Reader of the University.

The first meeting of Radical Orthodoxy had taken place only a few months before, in late July, around an ambiguous manifesto which was variously presented as humorous, ironic, or in earnest, and many in the Cambridge theological community either attended, or understood themselves excluded. Radical Orthodoxy has, from the outset, worked through 'insides' and 'outsides'. Lash, the first Catholic to hold a professorial chair in theology in either of the ancient English universities since the Reformation, began by saying "I am going to be rude about John Milbank", and offered only two mitigations: the need to meet Milbank's "energetically erudite polemic" with a "countervailing pugnacity"; and "the disagreements that I want to register are set in a much vaster context of agreement and respect".[2]

---

1  A distinction has been made throughout this volume between the book *Radical Orthodoxy: A New Theology*, edited by John Milbank, Catherine Pickstock, and Graham Ward, London, Routledge, 1999 (1998), referred to as *Radical Orthodoxy* (italics), and the 'movement' (unitalicised) of Radical Orthodoxy.
2  For the published text, see Lash, N., *Where Does Holy Teaching Leave Philosophy? Questions on Milbank's Aquinas* in *Modern Theology* October 1999, Vol. 15, No. 4, p. 433. The paper has been little, if at all, amended.

The discussions presented in this book continue that debate, and from much the same perspective. Few would question the excitement *Radical Orthodoxy* has brought to areas of theological debate in Britain since its publication. The sheer number of review articles, and their occasional acerbity, are testimony enough. More questionable, and fruitfully so, have been Radical Orthodoxy's (the movement's) assumptions, claims, and methods. This has been its genius, forcing otherwise treasured presuppositions out into the space of open debate.

The chapters in this volume spring from one such debate, a conference held at Heythrop College in June 1999, at which all three editors of *Radical Orthodoxy* generously entered into dispute with one Anglican and four Roman Catholic theologians. The exchanges, lively, and keenly argued, were marked by mutual sympathy and regard. Again the place of meeting was packed, this time with faculty members and graduates from mainly British (some North American, and one French) institutions. The same respectful rudeness re-emerged, now replicated in this text.[3] It is a rudeness Radical Orthodoxy invites: its refusal to be apologetic (itself an apologetic stance), its pugnacity, and its seemingly unshakeable convictions of inerrancy, all function as stimuli to debate, if correctly understood. These postures force the interlocutor's response, but they force her or him to think before responding. Self-conspection is the stuff of wiser thinking; challenges of this kind, though rough gymnastics mentally, nevertheless are generosity in disguise. If, in the course of replying, the original thesis is exploded, both *provocateur* and respondent grow with the result.

Anyone who has taught, or been taught, in the British universities of Oxford and Cambridge, or indeed at Heythrop (where we employ a similar method) will recognise this technique. It is the method of tutorial teaching, of closeting one or two undergraduates for an hour with their written essay and a teacher skilled in the matter at hand. The debate between Lash and Milbank was in many ways no more than this; fifty of us witnessed a tutorial at the highest degree, as if a master were pressing his brightest pupil to a higher

---

3  The tone of the debate was sharply reported by Margaret Hebblethwaite in an article in the British Catholic weekly *The Tablet*. The issues under discussion were, quite coincidentally, better summed up in an article on the Encyclical letter *Fides et Ratio* in the same edition of the journal by John Montag (a contributor to *Radical Orthodoxy*), *Philosophy's Human Face*. (Cf. *The Tablet*, June 19, 1999.)

wisdom. You may judge Lash's inspirational success for yourself: Milbank's later reply, published under the title *Intensities*, attempts to deal with his critic point for point.[4] At a time when adversarial debate, and adversity in struggling for better understanding (scholarly or otherwise) are poorly understood or valued, Radical Orthodoxy represents a certain freshness. The error, on our part or theirs, is to mistake gymnastic feats for truth. The gymnasium is a place of simulation; it prepares for obstacles and hardships to be faced beyond the schoolroom if wisdom is truly to be gained; else it is all prowess and pretiosity.

We must put this whole debate in its wider contexts. There is an emerging Catholic theological voice in Britain, of an unusual stamp. Unlike North America, we have no Catholic Universities here. Heythrop College, whose counter-reformation origins as a Jesuit seminary for England (founded in Belgium, at a time when none such was possible, on pain of death, on English soil) is the closest we have yet come, briefly having been a Pontifical Athenæum before finding our current home in the University of London. The Catholic contributors to this book reflect well the spread of Catholics in the academy in Britain; if you would expect to find a Dominican and a Jesuit, so also a secular cleric and, more often now, a lay-person. Most of us, lay or ordained, work in secular or secularised institutions. The debate between Lash and Milbank was more possible in Britain than in many other lands: these two were, after all, members of the same Faculty of Divinity.

Although Cambridge is the birthplace of Radical Orthodoxy, the conference which was pretext for this book took place on Heythrop's site in London. London is a place of harsher contrasts than Cambridge; a city of extraordinary cultural and social diversity. The postmodern is not only here to be speculatively observed, but is played out in its full euphoria and horror. The capital of 'Cool Britannia' boasts amongst the fastest growing incidence of infant tuberculosis in the Western world.

This book is organised in five sections, of which only this first, *Introduction*, is new. Each of the other four reports a conversation that took place on the day of the conference, under a specific title. The chapters in each section thereby form a unity. The *Introduction* adds an important comment from a Catholic perspective of Radical Orthodoxy's emergence on the North American stage. David Burrell, surely one of the finest and most widely

4   Milbank, J., *Intensities*, in *Modern Theology*, October 1999, Vol. 15, No. 4.

respected English-speaking minds in this area of theology, has undertaken his task with characteristic generous acuity.   His contribution highlights the differences in the academic situations of North America and Britain, in theology, and amongst Catholics especially.   If the middle three sections demonstrate the breadth of engagement of the editors of *Radical Orthodoxy*, the replies that match them show to good effect the emerging British Catholic voice I have indicated.  This voice, well featured by Oliver Davies and Fergus Kerr and further exemplified in James Hanvey's concluding section, demonstrates its historical perspicacity and close integration with, and understanding of, European Catholic scholarship.   One important voice amongst these Romans is Lucy Gardner's.  Stemming from the same High Anglicanism as Radical Orthodoxy, she nevertheless indicates the extent to which theirs is not yet the bespoke voice for their Anglo-Catholic roots.

Who is Radically Orthodox?   At various times, quite a number have participated in Radical Orthodoxy meetings. *Radical Orthodoxy* had twelve contributors in total, though not all (myself included) could comfortably take the label 'Radically Orthodox'.   The editors included a diversity of viewpoints, but not always so comfortably that diversity passed without comment.[5]  On the day of the Heythrop conference, and in the pages here, the three editors refer only to each other as 'Radically Orthodox', or tangentially to (the same) one other contributor to *Radical Orthodoxy*.  I would therefore suggest that Radical Orthodoxy the 'movement' may have wider supporters, but is foremost the editors of the book itself.  Even here, there are significant differences in approach: compare, for example, Graham Ward's contribution with John Milbank's.

Individually, and now collectively, they are a formidable force in the English-speaking debate concerning theology and culture.  John Milbank is the author of *Theology and Social Theory* and *The Word Made Strange*[6] as well as numerous articles.  Catherine Pickstock has authored *After Writing:*

---

5   Gavin D'Costa notes that "there is a revisionist prefacing of Loughlin's essay in the *Introduction* [to *Radical Orthodoxy*]". (D'Costa, G., *Seeking after Theological Vision* in *Reviews in Religion and Theology*, November 1999, Vol. 6, No. 4, p. 358). There is also a cautionary note introducing my interpretation of Heidegger (*Radical Orthodoxy*, p. 9).

6   Milbank, J., *Theology and Social Theory*, Oxford, Blackwell, 1990; *The Word Made Strange*, Oxford, Blackwell, 1997.

*The Liturgical Consummation of Philosophy*[7] and Graham Ward has written on Barth and Derrida, Religion and Critical Theory, as well as edited *The Postmodern God* and *The de Certeau Reader*.[8] He, too, has produced a considerable number of journal contributions.

Of the twelve contributors to *Radical Orthodoxy*, seven are Anglican, but five are Roman Catholic. In this sense, although routinely classed a High Anglican project, it is also more than this, as Fergus Kerr has noted.[9] If this volume represents a Catholic enquiry into *Radical Orthodoxy*, it does not do so as a disputation where theses are ranged, defended and attacked. Indeed, if my analysis below is correct, no single thesis could successfully mark the difference between a Catholic and a Radically Orthodox position.

Radical Orthodoxy, neither the book nor the purported movement, can be explained simply: it operates through a double-sidedness. In the first place, it does indeed seek to re-state a powerful Trinitarian and Christological orthodoxy, largely by appeal to Catholic authors. Its resources for doing so can hardly fail to impress. It achieves this orthodox position, however, by an entirely postmodern performance and citation. That there *are* two sides or faces of Radical Orthodoxy explains why so often criticism has failed to dent its self-confidence or that of its supporters. Unless the critique simultaneously shows how both sides are at work, it addresses only one; every critique of one side of *Radical Orthodoxy* can be deflected by moves made from the other.

If *Radical Orthodoxy* makes a strong appeal to Catholic scholarly resources, and above all the work of Augustine, Anselm, and Aquinas, we must question how it does so. *Radical Orthodoxy* has been criticised for its failure to address the question of its ecclesiology. Gavin D'Costa has observed that although both Catholics and Anglicans contributed to *Radical Orthodoxy*, yet "neither of these ecclesial communities ever make their real presence felt ... it is a church theology, with no 'accountability' to any real

---

7   Pickstock, C., *After Writing: The Liturgical Consummation of Philosophy*, Oxford, Blackwell, 1998.

8   Ward, G.: *Barth, Derrida, and the Language of Theology*, Cambridge, Cambridge University Press, 1995; *Theology and Contemporary Critical Theory*, London, Macmillan, 1996; *The Postmodern God: A Theological Reader*, Oxford, Blackwell, 1997; *The de Certeau Reader*, Oxford, Blackwell, 1999.

9   Kerr, F., *A Catholic Response to the Programme of Radical Orthodoxy*, p. 47.

church".[10]  Whereas D'Costa has properly discerned a reluctance to address the question of the Church amongst at least some of *Radical Orthodoxy*'s authors, he is, I believe, wrong to diagnose there is no ecclesiology at work in the movement.  A Catholic contributing to *Radical Orthodoxy* could assume that what he (no woman chose to contribute) wrote would be taken as within the frame of Catholic concerns.  The ecclesial question was implicit, but no less present for all that; an important indication of the possibilities available in the current ecumenical situation in Britain.

The question is not so simple for the three Anglican editors.  What can it mean for Anglicanism that Milbank has routinely appealed to Anselm, Augustine and Aquinas with only the explanation that they are the antidote to Scotus and the deformations (philosophical, yes, but surely theological as well) that followed; or that Pickstock has written extensively on the doctrine of transubstantiation[11] and the Latin Mass of the Council of Trent,[12] without particularly raising, for instance, that both transubstantiation and the Latin Mass were disavowed and condemned in Anglicanism's origins?[13]

Rusty Reno has argued that Radical Orthodoxy inherits an ecclesiology where "predominant Anglican practice could not provide an adequately rich catholic tradition, and the Roman Church, as currently constituted, could not provide an adequate institutional basis for faithfulness to the catholic tradition. Therefore a tradition had to be invented.  Of course, the invention was denied".[14]  Colin Gunton has, also from a reformed perspective, drawn attention to "weaknesses" of ecclesiological treatment, concluding "these authors behave as if the Reformation is of no more than tangential relevance

---

10 D'Costa, G., *Seeking after Theological Vision* in *Reviews in Religion and Theology*, November 1999, Vol. 6, No. 4, p. 358.

11 See, for instance, Pickstock C.: *Thomas Aquinas and the Quest for the Eucharist* in Beckwith, S. (ed.), *Catholicism and Catholicity, Eucharistic Communities in Historical and Contemporary Perspectives*, Oxford, Blackwell, 1999, esp. pp. 62-67; *Transubstantiation as the Condition of Possibility of All Meaning* in *After Writing*, pp. 259-261.

12 In *After Writing*, esp. ch. 4, *I Will Go Unto the Altar of God: The Impossible Liturgy*. Pickstock writes routinely of "the Mediæval Roman Rite", by which she clearly intends the post-reformation standardisation of the 1570 *Missale Romanum* of Pope Pius V.

13 See, for instance, the *Thirty-Nine Articles of Religion* of 1571, introduced by Act of Parliament and appended to the 1662 edition of the *Book of Common Prayer*: cf. Articles XXVIII and XXXI. Transubstantiation is described as "repugnant to the plain words of scripture" whilst the Mass is a "blasphemous fable".

14 Reno, R. R., *The Radical Orthodoxy Project* in *First Things*, February 2000.

to theology".[15] I am not asking whether they have the right to do this (which is outside my entitlement to comment); rather, my question is how will what they write be received in contexts where Catholic doctrinal formulations are contested? It is here that D'Costa's question of accountability is of issue.

When Catholics write of transubstantiation, or the dogma of the Assumption of the Mother of God, or the understanding of sacrifice implied in the Mass, we speak to, within, the *ecclesia*, or assembly, where these things are specifically taken to be true. When non-Catholics speak of the same things, they do so in ecclesial contexts which do not receive these doctrines in the same way. I do not even want to say that these doctrines are matters solely of Catholic concern – ecumenism demands that we Christians address the matter of our doctrinal formulations across the boundaries that divide us. To speak of these doctrines *un*-self-referentially (that is, without reference to the boundaries that contain *us*), however, is as Gunton, D'Costa, and others have suggested, to do something very strange indeed.

Surely, however, Radical Orthodoxy can respond by arguing that the consideration of Christian Doctrine in theology is legitimate matter for the academy? Entirely so, if Christian or Religious *studies* were at issue, and not Christian orthodoxy. While the academy may be one place of debate concerning Christian orthodoxy, it cannot be its place of legitimation, especially in Britain, where theology faculties have no really formal ecclesial affiliation, or the United States, where non-Catholic Schools are rarely under Church controls. To concede that the academy might legitimate or sanction the practice or convictions of believers (as opposed simply to discussing them) would be to concede everything to the secularisation that Radical Orthodoxy so fervently resists, and to make their own academician voice into a bid for authorial power within the academy itself.

Are not, however, the figures of Anselm, Aquinas and Augustine (especially as they are pre-reformation Christian thinkers) as much – if not more – of academic than ecclesial interest? Aquinas is a case in point, for as I argue elsewhere in this volume, his place in the Catholic Church is now held in consequence of its restoration through a Papal act of 1879. This is not to say that without Leo XIII's Encyclical Letter *Æterni Patris* Aquinas' work would have remained in the archives (though it might well), but rather that any

15 Gunton, G., *Editorial* in *International Journal of Systematic Theology*, July 1999, Vol. 1, No. 2, p. 117.

subsequent appeal to Aquinas cannot ignore or overlook the particular legitimacy his thought has been accorded in the schools of Thomism and what followed them.[16]

Without the restoration of Aquinas, it is doubtful, for instance, that Barth would have written in quite the way he did. What of Augustine and Anselm? To separate them from the ecclesial traditions of interpretation in which they variously stand is to associate them with what Stephen Sykes once described as "quinquesæcularism, the doctrine that the unanimous consent of the first five centuries contain all that the churches need to know about the faith, with neither deviation nor accretion", where the century referred has (for Anselm's or Aquinas' sake) simply been shifted to the Eleventh, Twelfth, or Thirteenth centuries.[17] This was the position clung to by the Oxford Movement of the Nineteenth century, and its ecclesiology is savagely summed up by Sheridan Gilley when he says that "they ended up believing in every doctrine of the Church except the doctrine of the Church. They lacked a convincing living authority, and therefore lived on past authority, invoking the decisions of the past undivided Church of the first five or ten Christian centuries".[18] To concede this, surely, would be for Radical Orthodoxy to concede the charge of nostalgia made against it, in that Sykes' point is that quinquesæcularism (and its variants) was always a worthy fiction, employed strategically to legitimate other concerns.[19]

Yet Radical Orthodoxy has performed an important service, in being part of the movement to return philosophical thought to its proper place in theology. Take, for instance, the doctrine of transubstantiation. If this neglected doctrine of the Church has been importantly re-examined in France

---

16  Leo XIII, Encyclical Letter *Æterni Patris*, Vatican, Libreria Editrice Vaticana, 1879.
17  Sykes, S. W., *Vision and Voting: Reflections on the Anglican Doctrine of the Church*, a lecture delivered in Oxford in 1993, published as *Foundations of an Anglican Ecclesiology* in *Living the Mystery: Affirming Catholicism and the Future of Anglicanism*, John, J. (ed.), Darton, Longman, and Todd, 1994, p. 39.
18  Gilley, S., *The Oxford Movement Reconsidered* in Cornwell, P. (ed.), *Prejudice in Religion*, London, Geoffrey Chapman, 1997, p. 27. From the Lent Lectures in St. James, Piccadilly, London, in 1995.
19  This is an accusation made, or at least raised, by a number of review articles, and replied to in Catherine Pickstock's chapter in this volume. (Cf. for just two examples: Hyman, G. in *New Blackfriars*, September 1999, Vol. 80, No. 943, p. 425; Jones, G., *On Not Seeing the Joke* in *Times Literary Supplement [TLS]*, 2nd April, 1999, p. 12.)

(in particular by Jean-Luc Marion and Louis-Marie Chauvet),[20] Radical Orthodoxy has played an important role in raising its discussion in English-speaking circles. It has routinely been supposed that transubstantiation 'fails' because of its dependence on the Aristotelian categories of substance and accident, a view which is entirely false, a reality only now being recovered.[21] In exactly the way I suggested earlier, this bringing to the fore of previous questions so that a higher understanding may be gained is Radical Orthodoxy's genius. In consequence of their broad reach, the important background work in Aristotle and Aquinas being undertaken by a diversity of scholars named in other chapters of this book, as well as some not named, has entered a more popular domain.[22]

This popularity has been in consequence of what Catherine Pickstock has explained in her contribution: "Radical Orthodoxy is a hermeneutic disposition and a style of metaphysical vision; and it is not so much a 'thing' or 'place' as a 'task'".[23] Whilst reviewers have repeatedly drawn attention to the difficulties of the texts that take the name of Radical Orthodoxy, they have been motivated to do so in the knowledge that they have been far more widely read than is normal for work of this stamp. Many have been surprised by the breadth of take-up of these densely argued texts, not least the editors themselves. Certainly in this volume there will be little enough light relief for the reader.

Styles, however, are never simply selected, but rather constitute their bearers. They are citations, abstracted from their material contexts and through mental intellection, represented on the surface of their stylists. Indeed, this is the very process Catherine Pickstock describes as Aquinas' "theory of the imagination"; it is in fact her own reproduction of Aquinas in

---

20 Marion, J-L., *Dieu sans l'être*, Paris, Librairie Arthème Fayard,1982 , Chapter 6; Chauvet, L-M., *Symbole et Sacrement*, Paris, Éditions du Cerf, 1987, p. 393 ff.

21 See my own discussion of this in *After Heidegger: Transubstantiation* in *Heythrop Journal*, April 2000, Vol. 41, No. 2.

22 Helen Lang, Professor at Trinity College, Connecticut, has over more than a decade been publishing critically important work on Aristotle and his reception in the Mediæval period of direct relevance to many of the discussions in this book. See Lang, H.: *Aristotle's Physics and its Medieval Varieties*, New York: SUNY Press, 1992; *The Order of Nature in Aristotle's Physics: Place and the Elements*, Cambridge, Cambridge University Press, 1998.

23 Pickstock, C., *Radical Orthodoxy and the Mediations of Time*, p. 62.

the formation of a style.[24] Style is the exteriorisation of imagination. It is what I see of your imagination when you have styled yourself for the sake of something, and I look at you. Styles act as forms of shorthand, explaining not simply through writing and being, but also the posture of what is written and borne, shortening the time needed to take their meaning in. Style is also a form of address, organising the response of its addressee by simultaneously inviting and repudiating – the very reason why Radical Orthodoxy has worked through 'outsides' and 'insides'. It is in this question of style that Radical Orthodoxy is at its most postmodern. Style is its genius and its peril: genius insofar as it forces recognition of the hidden in the familiar and perplexes its addressees; peril in that the instability of this perplexity leaves it open to misunderstanding, and concentrates attention too much on the shortcuts, rather than allowing what they are shortcuts to to appear.

Radical Orthodoxy's style explains two further issues raised in various places in this book: First, why there can be a lacuna between the persons of the editors of *Radical Orthodoxy* and their own repeated reference (and ours) to Radical Orthodoxy 'the movement'.[25] The unitalicised form is not, I suggest, an objectification, but rather a 'persona'. The persona of Radical Orthodoxy is *performed*, in ways I examine below. Second, there is the issue of Radical Orthodoxy's lack of self-reflexivity. If Radical Orthodoxy's appeal to Catholic doctrine has been largely un-self-referential, it has thereby exposed the need for self-reflexion in all thinking, including theology.

By self-reflexivity, I mean that taking account of myself as what philosophy is: what Aristotle understood as the relation between (what has later been named as 'practical' and 'speculative' wisdom) φρονήσις and σοφία, as philosophy's actual task. Not only do I seek to know, but I include myself in, and subject myself to the very enquiry through which knowledge and wisdom are gained. Σοφία is really wisdom taken for its own sake,

---

24  Pickstock, C., *Radical Orthodoxy and the Mediations of Time*, p. 71. She continues: "Briefly, then, what is the movement of human knowledge? When we seek to know a concrete singular thing, let us say a cricket bat, the form of the bat leaves its substance and becomes an abstract species. It travels through the human senses, then through the imagination, and finally into the mind of the observer". Pickstock here confuses matter with substance, for substance is always abstracted; intellection is a necessary condition of substance. (Cf. Aquinas, *In Libros Metaphysicorum*, I, Lect. 1; Aristotle, *Metaphysics* XII, esp. 1 and 5.)

25  See note 1 above.

wisdom which constantly interrogates the one who would be wise as his or her practice of *self*-interrogation, where the self puts itself at risk, in order to see more deeply and without error.

The adoption of a style can be the exteriorisation of this self-reflexion, or rather Radical Orthodoxy's self-reflexivity appears absent only because it is inscribed as the perceptible surface of the "metaphysical vision" it projects. It is to be *seen* as the style that it is. This is why Radical Orthodoxy is always able to collapse philosophy and theology into each other and proclaim they are the same. They are unified into a style that is *borne*.[26] The argumentation that preceded the inscription is hidden, for the sake of presenting the results. This, surely, is what 'poetics' is intended to mean. Radical Orthodoxy does not lead us into how to "rethink the tradition", rather it presents us with a vision of what the tradition looks like when it has been *re-thought*.[27]

The style of Radical Orthodoxy also explains its ecclesiology. The Church is the place where I am what I am truly called to be. Above all, in the Eucharist of the baptised, I assume the form I will have at the end of time. It is for this reason that the Church is constituted pneumatologically, from the future, and in fact from the end of time. In this way, the Church is my own exteriorisation (but as a place); an exteriorisation constituted from the future, therefore temporal in character, in a place shared with others. I cannot take a style here, for what I am to be is now only partially understood by me, and remains really unknown, and in God. Everything I *am* is disrupted, to be fulfilled for what I will *become*. Because this future is hidden and mysterious, it can never be closed off to reveal itself as a surface, or the borders and limit of a thing. For a style, however, what I am to become is announced through who I actually am now, but only because who I am is presented as a conditional face or mask, a style that presents me *as if* I were what I want you to see I have become. What I 'become' is fully projected on who I am for so

---

26 It might be objected here that styles have long existed in the Church, for instance in Religious Congregations, or in the way that von Balthasar speaks of styles of lay and clerical life in *Herrlichkeit*, Einsiedeln, Johannes Verlag, 1962, Vols. 2 and 3. This exactly begs the question of how style is legitimated and why (see below). Styles in religious life are legitimated through the *ecclesia*, and ultimately in the person of a Bishop or the Pope. They are authored ecclesially and lived out. For Radical Orthodoxy, style is not authored ecclesially, but subjectivally: *self*-authored as a "metaphysical vision". Style in this sense is not lived, but projected, as a function of the imaginary. The openness of the future ('what if ...') is closed off: *this* is what, 'if ...'.

27 Cf. *Radical Orthodoxy*, p. 2.

long as I adopt the style. It becomes me, as a style of clothing might suit, or become, me. The style is my exteriority, but it is a place where only I can be. This is not a place opened out by its futurity: in its immediacy, it is not a place at all, but a surface. It cannot be shared, it can only be copied.

A style, as Nietzsche explains through the personæ he invents to 'speak' his philosophical thought, is not a real person, but the metaphysical structure of a person. It is what a person *would* be 'if' they really were the mask they represent. If producing a theology as a style is fundamentally Radical Orthodoxy's genius, it brings with it attendant dangers.

Martin Heidegger understood the collapse of philosophy into theology as a consequence of the 'end' of metaphysics. Something will emerge, he suggests, where theology becomes styles of theology or 'theologies', which have no responsibility toward God at all, but reduce God to the kind of commodity that technology routinely manipulates. Theology thereby becomes "diabology", in that it is cut off from discussing God as God, because God is reduced now only to a commodity to be traded either in mere conceptualisations or in their encapsulation in things.[28] The clear inference is that theology, whilst claiming to speak of God, ends up juggling names and concepts. Books and the published word, whose relations are now entirely ordered through the concerns of publishers and through endlessly manipulable media, become the commodified encapsulations of these names. *Différance* explains well the violence of the gap that opens up between what I write and how it is disseminated, remembering that the whole panoply of commodity distribution of marketable objects is implied here as well. Heidegger indicates how the love of God can be packaged as no more than a brand name.

One word that has made an appearance in the chapters of this volume, and that may go some way to explain what is unfolding in the issue of style and

---

28 Heidegger, M., *Metaphysik und Nihilismus* in *Gesamtausgabe*, Frankfurt, Klostermann, 1999, Vol. 67, *Das Zeitalter der »Theologien«*, §145, p. 154 f. (From a text written between 1938 and 1939.) "Im Zeitalter des Endes aller Metaphysik ... (wird) die Theologie zur *Diabologie*, die ... erst unbedingte Unwesen Gottes in die Wahrheit des Seienden ein- und losläßt." ["In the age of the end of all metaphysics, theology becomes *diabology*, which admits and unleashes the unconditional non-essence of God into the truth of beings."] "Unbedingte(s) Unwesen" is almost impossible to translate in this context, having the additional possible sense of 'absolutely dreadful state of affairs'. Clearly Heidegger is extrapolating from Nietzsche's devaluation of the uppermost values, where 'God' is 'reduced' as an objectified thing (value) in order to be the uppermost value.

ecclesiology, is 'performance'. Not once, but several times, reference has been made to the 'performance' by Radical Orthodoxy of Aquinas, or of its other canonical positions.[29] Performance and performativity are terms now often found in postmodern discourse. If their origins lie in analytic philosophy and in Wittgenstein,[30] they have come into contemporary discourse largely at the hands of Judith Butler and Eve Kosovsky Sedgewick.[31] Butler relocates performativity through her reading of Nietzsche. She cites "Nietzsche's claim in *On the Genealogy of Morals* that 'there is no "being" behind doing, effecting, becoming; "the doer" is merely a fiction added to the deed – the deed is everything'".[32]

Butler develops her argument, however, by analysing performativity through Nietzsche's elaboration of the 'will to power'. By performing *as* the powerful, power is thereby ascribed to the one performing. The paradox, often misunderstood when Butler is cited, is that the one perform*ing* is in fact more perform*ed as* or *by* what he or she performs. The ascription of power displaces identity and subverts it, as the displacement of identity displaces power for the sake of the performer in repeating it. Here is the explanation of what it means both to copy a style, and to be understood through the styles we perform. When I assume the clothing of the Judge, the apparatus of the state that legitimates my solemn judgement is simultaneously assumed, by being *seen* to be inscribed upon my person. This assumption of power can be legitimate or parodic, depending on whether I really am a judge, or simply act as *if*. In both cases, however, there is a relation to power.[33]

---

29 Milbank J., *The Programme of Radical Orthodoxy*, p. 34; Hemming, L., *Quod Impossibile Est! Aquinas and Radical Orthodoxy*, p. 92; Ward, G., *Radical Orthodoxy and/as Cultural Politics*, p. 100; Davies, O., *Revelation and the Politics of Culture*, p. 118 and p. 124; Gardner, L., *Listening at the Threshold*, p. 142 (note 44) and 163; Hanvey, J., *Conclusion*, p. 163.
30 Austin, J. L., *How to do Things with Words* in *Philosophical Papers*, Oxford, Oxford University Press, 1961 (1955), esp. pp. 233-252. Wittgenstein, L., *Philosophical Investigations*, translated by Anscombe, G. E. M., Oxford, Blackwell, 1958 (1953), I.
31 See Kosovsky Sedgewick, E., *Queer Performativity* in *GLQ*, Spring 1993, Vol. 1, No. 1; Butler J., *Gender Trouble*, London, Routledge, 1990, p. 24 f.; *Bodies that Matter*, London, Routledge, 1993, *passim*. See also Šišek, S., *The Plague of Phantasies*, New York, Verso, 1997, p. 150.
32 Butler, J., *Gender Trouble*, p. 25, citing Nietzsche, F., *Zur Genealogie der Moral*.
33 Wittgenstein also makes this point, and expressly ties its functioning to language. Wittgenstein, L., *Philosophical Investigations*, I, §426. "Die Ausdrucksweise scheint für einen Gott zugeschnitten zu sein, der weiß, was wir nicht wissen können; er sieht die

Butler refers to gender, but as theorists familiar with her work have understood, her understanding of the performative works well in all spheres where the question of power is posed. In fact performativity also well explains ascriptions of power made by humanity from the divine. In this sense 'the performative' is the postmodern name of 'participation'. This, after all, is the burden of Nietzsche's critique of both the will to power and the death of God; that reason, if it is understood to be regulatory even of the divine, is thereby idolised. Such idolatry is bound to be deposed, at the very point where the claims of an architectonic reason as a force regulative even of God are exposed as inadequate.[34] Why is this useful to us here, in understanding Radical Orthodoxy as performance? Butler notes:

> Discursive performativity appears to produce what it names, to enact its own referent, to name and to do, to name and to make. Paradoxically, however, this productive capacity of discourse is derivative, a form of cultural iterability or rearticulation, a practice of *re*signification, not creation ex nihilo. Generally speaking, a performative functions to produce that which it declares. As a discursive practice (performative 'acts' must be *repeated* to become efficacious), performatives constitute a locus of *discursive production*. No 'act' apart from a regularised and sanctioned practice can wield the power to produce that which it declares. Indeed a performative act apart from a reiterated and, hence, sanctioned set of conventions can appear only as a vain effort to produce effects that it cannot possibly produce.[35]

For the Catholics who contributed to *Radical Orthodoxy*, our appeal to Catholic doctrine could always be taken as regularised and sanctioned within

ganzen unendlichen Reihen und sieht in das Bewußtsein des Menschen hinein. Für uns freilich sind diese Ausdrucksformen quasi ein Ornat, das wir wohl anlegen, mit dem wir aber nicht viel anfangen können, da uns die reale Macht fehlt, die dieser Kleidung Sinn und Zweck geben würde." ["... the form of expression we use seems to have been designed for a god, who knows what we cannot know; he sees the whole of each of those infinite series and sees into human consciousness. For us, of course, these forms of expressions are like pontificals which we may put on, but cannot do much with, since we lack the effective power that would give these vestments meaning and purpose."]

34 Butler recognises this when she indicates the link between her understanding of gender and Nietzsche's critique of God. She says "The law (of sex) ... can be subject to the same kind of critique that Nietzsche formulated of the notion of God: the power attributed to this prior and ideal power is derived and deflected from the attribution itself." (Butler, J., *Bodies that Matter*, p. 14.)

35 Butler, J., *Bodies that Matter*, p. 107. (Author's italics.)

the *ecclesia*, to the point where such legitimation did not need to be claimed to be enacted. However, the editors of Radical Orthodoxy have also remained silent with regard to the legitimation of the doctrines and figures they reiterate. Uncritically, to re-perform Catholic dogma from without, however, in a context (ecclesial or academic) which cannot receive it, cannot, for the reasons Butler here explains, really produce the effects that are desired. On the other hand, to reiterate uncritically Catholic doctrine and figures, as Radical Orthodoxy has tended to do, deflects the power that sanctions and legitimates them, namely the unity of the Catholic Church, exemplified in the Petrine Office. It is no accident, therefore, that the only point at which the editors of *Radical Orthodoxy* attempt formally to distinguish themselves from Roman Catholicism is in the current character of the Petrine office itself.[36]

If Radical Orthodoxy is legitimated through the deflection of power, and if this power originates, as I have suggested, in the character of the Petrine office, surely my argument simply reinforces the power of power, which would concede everything to Nietzsche and nihilism, even affirming that power in the Church is an effect of *der Wille zur Macht*? Indeed, Radical Orthodoxy's own articulation of nihilism recognises that the question of power is sharply posed in postmodernity, but it has lacked the ability to resolve it. The question of power is everywhere posed in contemporary culture, including in the Church. Power, as Nietzsche well knew, both discloses limit and finitude in its lack, and yet in its enactment knows no limit. The question of power within the Church is now routinely confused with the question of authority, in an error that marks us deeply. This error is, at the deepest level, our (ecclesial) experience of nihilism itself.

Those of us who have admired the achievements of Radical Orthodoxy, and especially its editors, must hope that through its posing of difficult questions, above all to itself, it will find its way to a higher place. Catholic thinkers in Britain and in the United States as well, have sometimes been too apt to overlook or suppress our tradition: the powerful philosophical and historical as well as theological resources which form the basis of our self-

---

36 "In this way the designation 'orthodox' transcends confessional boundaries, since both Protestant biblicism and post-tridentine Catholic positivist authoritarianism are seen as aberrant results of theological distortions already dominant even before the early modern period" (*Radical Orthodoxy*, p. 2). It is difficult to see this reference to Catholicism in any other way than as referring to the Petrine office itself, and certainly to the power that it represents.

understanding and self-experience. Radical Orthodoxy, in being so willing to engage with Catholic sources and debate Catholic formulations of doctrine, issues us a timely warning: we forget what they have seen and returned to memory at our peril. The emerging Catholic voice in Britain is still small. More than one American theologian has lamented that Catholic scholars' neglect of philosophy and fundamental theology leads many of us to write and think in modes too much formed by the questionable epistemological and ontological assumptions of our age. This, too, is the ecclesial experience of nihilism.

If the question of the power of power is also posed by Radical Orthodoxy, then the question as I have asked it is really what should both Radical Orthodoxy, and the debate this book represents, be striving towards? If, as I have suggested, Radical Orthodoxy's genius is to pose questions that lead to their own self-overcoming, how will this be? Pope John Paul II recently reminded us that power in the Church is to be understood in the following way: "it is to the holiness of the faithful that the hierarchical structure of the Church is totally ordered".[37] Holiness is the only legitimate power that the *ecclesia* knows, for it is the only legitimate experience of the power of God, both from within and without. The theologian, participating in the teaching office of the Church, and assisting the *ecclesia* to divine the times, is in part to discern the yearning for redemption that is present in culture. This means that theology is always required to understand itself as a pastoral task. Theology must deepen reflection for the sake of the lived life of faith, which means it must serve the faithful who strive for a deeper self-understanding and greater holiness. In this sense the theologian is him- and herself similarly ordered to the holiness of the faithful, and so called also to be holy.

What is holiness, but the depth of existential sharing in the passion of Christ? What most nihilates power, but self-negation for the sake of revealing who God might be? Surely at the heart of this lies a profound meditation on the Cross, the well-spring of sanctity itself? Sanctity can also be (inversely) understood as the transgression of the performative, as the annihilation of style for the sake of interior grace. Eadmer, the biographer of Anselm, tells us that his sainted father's desire for God was "that his own life might not be at

---

37  John Paul II, Apostolic Letter *Sacerdotalis Ordinatio*, Vatican, Libreria Editrice Vaticana, 1994, §3. "Ceterum ad fidelium sanctitatem funditus ordinatur hierarchica Ecclesiæ constitutio."

variance with his speech and writings".[38]  This is the mirror image and annihilation of the difference that postmodernity asserts that writing is, and that Radical Orthodoxy analyses as nihilism (especially when speaking of Jacques Derrida), all for the sake of Anselm's growth in Christ.

Who we are through grace is Christ, with the limitation that to be in Christ is always simultaneously distant from (in sin and separation) and close to (through the means of redemption) Christ – that I must always take my very self into account for the sake of the one whom I long to reveal, both to myself and in the world.  Self-reflection lies at the heart of faith.  Christ is not a style; we live in Christ, and insofar as we do, we are open to the redemption offered us through Christ.  If I am the place where Christ is revealed for myself, and if I am to be a place of revelation of Christ to the world, I am also what obscures the revelation.  To reveal Christ I must be crucified to self, which means (in a more modern idiom) I must also point the way to the abandonment of every pretension to power, of my own and others.  I cannot, therefore, perform Christ.  Christ is no persona, in whom I live as 'if ...', but rather Christ, and *alter Christus*, is the real person whom I must become, but am always not yet.  The distance always throws *me* into relief, so that I am always aware of who I am insofar as I am like Christ, and insofar as I am not, and still more, that the extent to which I am separate from Christ remains unknown to me.  To all of this is the theologian called.

We can only applaud the continuing efforts to return philosophy to its proper place in theological discourse, called for by John Paul II in *Fides et Ratio* and reflected in much of Radical Orthodoxy's work.  We must not forget, however, that philosophy – for Aristotle, for Aquinas, and in the more recent statements of *Fides et Ratio*, is for the sake of, not reason, strictly speaking (the architectonic, calculative, scientific reason of the Enlightenment), but wisdom.  Wisdom alone can deepen the gift of faith, when given.

---

38 "Inter hæc cum iam ut dictis et scriptis suis mores sui in nullo doscordarent ..." Eadmer, *Vita Sancti Anselmi*, (c. 1125), translated as *The Life of St. Anselm* by Southern, R. W., London, Nelson's Medieval Texts, 1962, p. 35 (34).

Chapter Two

# Radical Orthodoxy
# in a
# North American Context

David B. Burrell CSC

I have been asked to comment on the reception of the programme which calls itself Radical Orthodoxy in the North American context, and to do so from a Catholic point of view. Ever since my introductory review[1] of John Milbank's *Theology and Social Theory* I have been fascinated by the way in which his writings and those of others, notably Catherine Pickstock, have challenged both the insular character of theological inquiry as well as the presumed division of labour between philosophy and theology. Some philosophers of religion in America have contested that divide as well, proceeding to investigate traditionally theological topics with more explicit philosophical tools.

Yet their inquiries have largely been conceived as corrective of a theology which they tend to regard as having 'lost its nerve', nor do their methods display the requisite instruction in the history of Christian thought to be taken as bona fide theological explorations. Moreover, aside from such apologetic forays into theological domains, staunchly Christian philosophers of religion in North America have rather been concerned to employ current philosophical strategies to claim legitimacy for their overly religious inquiries than they have been conscious of ways in which such strategies might effectively undermine those very efforts – by precluding, for example, a rendering of divinity that would be properly transcendent. And yet it is just such a critique which proponents of Radical Orthodoxy have been mounting, tracing the origins of a modernist approach back to Scotus' predilection for univocity, and

---

1 Burrell, D., *An Introduction to Theology and Social Theory: Beyond Secular Reason*, in *Modern Theology*, October 1992, Vol. 8, No. 4.

what motivated his rejection of the inherently analogous character of 'being'.[2] Rather than see postmodern thought-forms as offering the opportunity for a fresh approach to traditional questions of philosophical theology, these philosophers of religion would rather keep such 'continental' forays at arm's length; their interlocutors lie elsewhere. What, then, of theologians in North America? An adequate reply to that question requires some extensive reflection on the way in which the social location of theologians in America cannot but influence the issues they deem worth their time and effort, as well as the way to approach them.

In North America, theology can be pursued as an academic subject in seminaries, university divinity schools, and departments of theology in church-related colleges and universities. Public institutions have long regarded the teaching of theology as breaching the time-honoured 'separation of church and state', while most independent colleges, as well as universities without divinity schools attached, have followed the inclination of the academy to regard theology as failing to meet the litmus tests of 'objective' inquiry, and hence inappropriate as a subject of study.

Many of these institutions have come to recognise the need for 'religious studies', and a few such departments even make room for theological inquiry, though the prevailing ethos remains the one outlined, which can find staunch defenders among 'religious studies' faculty members. (The argument, of course, is the familiar Enlightenment one that the faith-commitments demanded of theologians undermine their 'objectivity' in pursuing questions of divinity.) Needless to say, that leaves relatively few venues for serious study, with each of them missing some key features of that environment one might consider ideal for carrying out theological inquiry. For example, the overweening academic context of a university can easily impel the theologians operating within it towards a conversation preoccupied with their academic colleagues rather than one focused on the community of believers. While such efforts represent a noble endeavour, which might even be compared favourably with Aquinas' evidently pastoral concern to show how *theologia*

2 See Milbank's contribution to this volume, as well as his dialogue with Jean-Luc Marion in Milbank, J., *Only Theology Overcomes Metaphysics* in *The Word Made Strange*, Oxford, Blackwell, 1997; but see Marion's retraction: *Saint Thomas d'Aquin et l'onto-théo-logie* in *Revue Thomiste* 1995, No. 95. Catherine Pickstock makes a similar point in *After Writing: The Liturgical Consummation of Philosophy*, Oxford, Blackwell, 1998, pp. 121-29.

qualifies as *scientia*, it is easy to see how such an environment can lull the conversants into accepting a certain set of presuppositions while marginalising other perspectives of the kingdom of God.

What appears as a lacuna in university-based theology could become a crippling preoccupation in seminaries, however, where ecclesiastical issues can readily constrain the free-ranging character which theological inquiry needs to pursue its transcendent subject: God and the things of God. Of the 'things of God', moreover, theologians can also be enlisted to make social and political capital of 'identity-issues', especially as prospective ministers become acutely aware of the marginalisation of church in current American society, and seek for ways to make an impact as well as strengthen their own commitment to the kingdom. This can be especially true in undergraduate teaching, where instructors can become preoccupied with making theology 'relevant'. Yet the concerns of young people have shifted in that regard of late, as the emptiness of an aggressively secular society, despite its obvious blandishments, has impelled many of them to turn to faith-communities as vehicles for 'finding themselves' in the midst of a society whose commitments to the 'bottom line' leave little room for caring. Their palpable need for community inspires them to trace the expression of caring they find in faith communities to its roots in faith in God. Indeed, the pervasive 'loss of faith in reason' so emblematic of a postmodern sensibility can also open the way to regarding faith as a path to knowing, quite contrary to the 'modernist' set of assumptions which has characterised the ideology of 'religious studies'. (A few years ago I overheard a snatch of conversation between two students at the end of class, where she closed off debate by reminding him: "Haven't you heard atheism's out!").

Yet the desire for community can also express itself as a palpable need for certitude, so that faith can quickly become, for these young people, just what the Enlightenment feared it to be: a way of closing off further inquiry by holding onto formulæ which promise stability in the midst of surrounding chaos.

Bernard Lonergan's reminder that the world of inquiry divides between those who need certitude and those who seek for understanding proves to be of assistance here. While his manifest example was Descartes (and a re-reading of the *Discourse on Method* with that distinction in mind can allow one to see just how psychological a text it is), the distinction readily applies to the propensities towards 'fundamentalism' among people everywhere, and notably among young people at sea in an uncaring world of blandishments. Their deep inner alienation from that world, in which they are otherwise so completely at home, leads them to find the accommodationist strategies of 'liberal' theologians pointless, while their acquaintance with 'critical thought' in its standard academic guise can only reinforce Alasdair MacIntyre's dramatic scenario of endless and fruitless debate. In this way faith and faith-communities become a haven. It is precisely at this point, however, where Lonergan's distinction can gain purchase, and an agenda like that of *Radical Orthodoxy* will find a hearing. For the students whom I encounter are hardly uncritical, since their very schooling in critical modes of thinking has enabled them to come this far. What they miss, however, is the *point* of it all. And if their philosophical mentors display a face of critical reason which proves corrosive to any commitment at all, then all the other factors mentioned will conspire to impel them to prefer commitment at any cost, even that of critical reflection.

Therefore between a pointless display of eristic reason and a caring display of uncritical faith, they may readily prefer the latter. But true education cannot rest with preferences, so an authentic theology will be called upon to present an alternative to a consumer society which so easily infects the exercise of academe as well, and we find that the best way to do that is by critically appropriating the fullness of a faith-tradition.[3]

Before proceeding further, it is worth noting the direction these reflections have taken, for some may find that course quite tangential to the subject. Beginning with a set of reminders about the institutional contexts in which theology is carried out in North America, I began to speak about the sensibilities of students today, with particular attention to undergraduates and a sidelong glance at students for ministry. If these animadversions appear irrelevant to those ensconced in academic fields, it is that very myopia which they intend to challenge. In fact, the propensity of the academy to multiply sub-fields in order to assure practitioners a place on its competitive and often consumer-driven stage (see Boyle's pointed analysis in *Who are We Now?*)

3     Boyle, N., *Who are We Now?*, Edinburgh, T & T Clark, 1999, makes these points elegantly and incisively. The normative notion of a faith-tradition employed here is beholden to Alasdair MacIntyre's complementary studies: *Whose Justice? Which Rationality?*, Indiana, University of Notre Dame Press, 1988; and *Three Rival Versions of Moral Enquiry*, Indiana, University of Notre Dame Press, 1990.

proves to be one of the negative features of the modern university as a fruitful environment for doing theology. For we invariably find the most interesting topics to fall between these constructed sub-fields, as William Cavanaugh's recent book, *Torture and Eucharist* illustrates so well: if torture belongs to ethics and Eucharist to liturgy, how can they be treated together?[4] Of course, these complaints hardly refer to theology alone, as a recent review of assessments of the practices associated with the many-faceted discipline of English in American universities attests.[5] Yet does not that express the very intent of Radical Orthodoxy as well as its attraction: to explore intellectual inquiry at the service of a committed and critical faith-community as a way of challenging those Enlightenment presuppositions which have come to jeopardise inquiry itself? Moreover, it is crucial that one does *not* turn this movement (which it cannot help but be) into a "crusade" against the Enlightenment *tout court* (which any movement can too easily become), for any faith-tradition will need, for its very authenticity, the legacy of critical thinking which the Enlightenment at its best represents.[6] So Radical Orthodoxy will require that internal relation between faith and reason which its best proponents display, and which John Paul II has urged in his recent *Fides et Ratio*.

In fact, the insulation endemic to any institutional context may well explain how most of those engaged in the teaching of theology in North America might fail to appreciate the challenges of Radical Orthodoxy. (A recent review of theological journals by the editor of *Theological Studies*, arguably the journal most representative of theology in North America, canvassed those published in many languages yet failed even to notice *Modern Theology*, which has become the locus for perspectives congenial to Radical Orthodoxy.) Those ensconced in the academy may also have become so enamoured of the freedom that environment enjoys from ecclesiastical interference that they can easily overlook the constraints and myopia which that same milieu exercises over their pursuit of theological inquiry, while the social location of seminary teaching can often elicit an opposite hankering for a university milieu – though that is not universally true, as the remarkable work of Robert Barron

4   Cavanaugh, W., *Eucharist and Torture*, Oxford, Blackwell, 1999.
5   Delbanco, A., *The Death of Literature* in *New York Review of Books*, 4 November 1999, Vol. 46, No. 17.
6   Charles Taylor develops this reading in illuminating detail in his *Sources of the Self: The Making of the Modern Identity*, Massachusetts, Harvard University Press, 1989.

attests.[7] What is significant here, as we shall see, is the way in which 'church' can so easily be cast as the enemy, and so reinforcing in our universities an insouciance about the *telos* of theology in service of the kingdom of God, while engendering in seminaries an oppositional attitude in quest of elbow room for creative ministry.  As for doctoral students, they may also find themselves unable to respond to the challenge for two reasons: their training may ill equip them to negotiate the philosophical idiom in which the proposals of *Radical Orthodoxy* are regularly cast, while their concern to establish themselves professionally may tempt them to adapt to the worldview of their professors, despite misgivings about those very perspectives.  In short, they may not be able to afford to recognise a myopia which may nonetheless discomfort them.

We return, therefore, to undergraduates, our only 'disinterested' students, in the appropriate sense of being able to follow the arguments without self-interest interfering, and so able to register their dissatisfaction as well as their delight in finding ways to elucidate matters divine.

One way of recognising the import of institutional milieux and of student attitudes in shaping theological inquiry is to see them reflecting the ways in which authentic traditions are ever assimilative, and especially those traditions explicitly based on a revelation.  For what exploits the resources of the original revelation, making it truly revelatory to each generation, is the continuing commentary.  Those of us engaged in inter-faith inquiry and comparative theology have found ourselves guided by the prescient reflections of Jean Daniélou in the fifties, in his two little books, *Salvation of Nations* and *Advent*.[8]  Contrasting the ideology of 'the missions' with the fruitful practice of mission in lands outside the historic purview of Christendom, he suggested that we replace thinking of missionaries as "bringing Christ to India" (since they inevitably brought Portugal with them!) with seeing them finding him there.  Radical as this may initially sound, it more accurately parses their practice, since attempting to expound the truth of the gospel to those formed in other religious cultures inevitably elicits questions which will reveal

---

7   See Barron, R., *Now I See*, New York, Crossroads, 1998, which develops the potential of doctrinal statements to become "food for the soul", as well as his synthesis of the philosophical and spiritual dimensions of Aquinas' life and work, in his *Thomas Aquinas: Spiritual Master*, New York, Crossroads, 1995.
8   Daniélou, J., *Salvation of Nations*, New York and London, Sheed and Ward, 1958; *Advent*, New York and London, Sheed and Ward, 1958.

hitherto unsuspected faces of the Christ one came to communicate. In these same terms, however, mission has come to embrace exchange with alien environments at home, so that every attempt to 'teach theology' will involve a fresh discovery of one's tradition and with that a new face of the Christ who is our revelation. Again, is not that the reason why 'retrieving the tradition' must be endemic to the teaching of theology, and can never be mere repetition or a vain restoration, but always discovering something new? This is the sense in which Radical Orthodoxy does well to acknowledge its lineage with the *nouvelle théologie* of mid-century Catholic thought, as John Milbank does in his contribution to this volume, yet it will perforce reflect the fresh set of concerns which he delineates.

The undergraduate students to whom I keep returning, however, will hardly be cognisant of these concerns, embedded as they are in the dialectic of theology's historical unfolding. What they will resonate with, however, is the critical exposition of the tradition which this fresh start urges and initiates. They will also appreciate its being done comparatively, since they find themselves increasingly in conversation with people of other faiths, and may even find more fruitful communication with them than with their ostensibly post-Christian contemporaries. In fact, just as *Radical Orthodoxy* received its initial impulse from finding in postmodernism "a moment of opportunity for theology, because it seemed to qualify and diminish secular claims to truth",[9] its quest for a space of "original peace" from which discourse might be directed to truth, instead of distracted into constant antagonism, may find fruitful direction from interfaith parallels which bring similar constructive critiques to bear on our current intellectual myopias.[10] But whether we gain perspective through a critical retrieval of our own traditions, or by discerning illuminating parallels in others, it is a fresh perspective which we need and which our students appreciate. My own experience with undergraduates would lead me to recommend the work of Sebastian Moore, whose writings are of course too poetic to let him be claimed as a mainstream theologian![11]

9    Milbank, J., *The Programme of Radical Orthodoxy*, p. 42 (below).
10   I have tried to do just that in Burrell, D., *Freedom and Creation in Three Traditions*, Indiana, University of Notre Dame Press, 1993, which tried to expose the inadequacies of our 'libertarian' constructions of human freedom in the light of the Abrahamic traditions' shared faith in the free creator of all that is.
11   Moore, S., *The Crucified Jesus is no Stranger*, New York, Crossroads, 1977, followed by *The Fire and the Rose are One*, New York, Crossroads, 1980, and *Jesus the Liberator of Desire*, New York, Crossroads, 1989.

I have already cited Robert Barron, and should also refer to the teaching of my colleague and confrère, John Dunne, reflected in his voluminous writings, which shares Sebastian Moore's poetic penchant. I cite these three as salient examples of North American counterparts of *Radical Orthodoxy*, in that they share its goals if not its prevailing method.[12]

While those who have contributed to giving this movement a name could hardly be accused of a poetic penchant, the mention of poetry in the same context as theology should alert us to other ways of making the kind of critique which Radical Theology proposes. If the tendency of the very thought forms of modernity is to embody a rejection of the world as created, as I would argue most of them tend to do, then seeking another mode of expression may well be a useful way of alerting us to that fact. Rather than appearing suspect, as doing theology 'poetically' inevitably will to the theological establishment, others of us who find that same establishment often standing in the way of authentically retrieving our theological tradition should welcome the way in which more poetic thinkers can open our eyes and ears to that distortion.

I have tried to suggest how social location can lead to an establishment mentality in executing any discipline, and the peculiar ways in which that has come to affect the doing of theology in North America. Yet while none of those milieux could easily espouse anything neither 'radical' nor 'orthodox', for the reasons adduced, I have also indicated how students today find themselves ripe for the very constructive critique which Radical Orthodoxy proposes. Yet the mode of executing that critique is so imbedded in intra-theological concerns that it can hardly address the very students who are seeking what it is proposing: a retrieval of a rich tradition in a manner which the contemporary intellectual climate calls for yet will certainly resist. At the same time, however, it is crucial that they be addressed, for otherwise their dissatisfaction with the explicitly uncommitted approaches of the 'religious studies' variety will tend to impel them towards an uncritical set of certitudes which will be offered to them as religious faith. So we stand at a crucial and fruitful moment in doing and teaching theology in North America. If I am myself sceptical of the capacities of academic theology to meet that moment,

---

12 Of John S. Dunne's many works, I would single out: *The Way of all the Earth*, London, Sheldon Press, 1973; *Time and Myth*, London, SCM Press, 1979 (1973); and *House of Wisdom*, London, SCM Press, 1985.

it may be that I have been associated with it too long, even in an administrative capacity. Yet there were few antecedents for this movement in Britain either, so hope should spring eternal for North America as well. And while I would carefully distinguish that hope from optimism, in the spirit of Nicholas Lash's *A Matter of Hope*, I might also suggest that a fruitful opening exists in the fledgling field of comparative theology, where a number of younger thinkers are perforce challenging current academic and theological boundaries to explore the Christian tradition in ways which should prove "mutually illuminating".[13]

On a concluding note, let me acknowledge my own social location, if only to warn readers that others could legitimately take other approaches to this topic. Moreover, in mentioning the particular theologians which I did, I can easily have overlooked others of cognate spirit, which indicates nothing more than my own limitations in executing so broad and demanding a mandate. In that same spirit, let me call attention more explicitly to the fact that my involvement with academic theology in a Catholic university context covers the time in which Catholic theologians sought to respond to Vatican II. My own theological education at the Gregorian between 1956 and 1960 with Bernard Lonergan and others had happily anticipated the church's appropriation in that council of the perspectives of the largely French *nouvelle théologie*, which explains my own appreciation and appropriation of Vatican II. Indeed I have often reflected that most of those Conciliar voices which the journalists called 'progressive' had in fact completed their doctoral studies in Patristics, so I had always seen Vatican II as disseminating to the churches a practice of retrieving a rich tradition, notably across what had become the massive divide of the sixteenth century.

I was subsequently moved by Karl Rahner's seminal lecture (in 1979) which regarded, in retrospect, the slim document *Nostra Ætate* to be the signal achievement of the council itself, in that it executed a salient step forward in the relation of Christianity to other religions of the world, and did so in ways

---

13  The phrase is Brad Malkowsky's, and also the work of Fredericks, J. L., *Faith among Faiths*, New York, Paulist Press, 1999; Clooney, F., *Theology after Vedanta: An Experiment in Comparative Theology*, Albany, SUNY, 1993, and Griffiths, P., *An Apology for Apologetics: A Study in the Logic of Interreligious Dialogue*, New York, Orbis, 1991, as well as his recent *Religious Reading*, New York, Oxford University Press, 1999.

quite unprepared by previous reflection.[14] Beyond these personal facts, however, lies an appreciation of Vatican II as a step backward as well as forward, if you will, at the same time, as theology must always be adept at executing. So one can only deplore a jejeune utilisation of that council as at once initiating and licensing an uncritical accommodation with modernity: a tactic which unfortunately became the stock in trade of some Catholic theologians, only to initiate a backlash from a new generation whose acquaintance with modernity has been considerably less felicitous.[15]

I have tried to identify some reasons why the strenuous programme of Radical Orthodoxy may not have found much resonance to date among Catholic theologians in North America. Peter Steinfels' identification of a "crisis of intellect" in what has come to be called 'liberal Catholicism' could offer another reason, however unflattering, since most academic theologians (and their major professional association, the Catholic Theological Society of America, CTSA) would fit that descriptive category.[16] The temptation of theologians, especially those immersed in a 'correlationist' model of inquiry, to adopt thought patterns ready-to-hand, would lead them to resist the trenchant deconstruction of modernist patterns of thought and discourse which Radical Orthodoxy proposes.

A similar penchant can be found in the current spate of writing in philosophy of religion, which seems more intent on putting the categories of analytic philosophy to a theological use than it is in querying how appropriate such categories may (or may not) be to the subject at hand. While this may sound disparaging of the theological scene in North America, I am nonetheless confident that most of the practitioners involved would not find these remarks to be critical of their efforts, since they would be reluctant to acknowledge any significant lacunæ in current practice. What we find is that analytic philosophers of religion share a set of presuppositions which tend to remain

---

14 Rahner, K., *Towards a Fundamental Interpretation of Vatican II*, in *Theological Studies*, December 1979, Vol. 40. *Nostra Ætate* in *Sacrosanctum Œcumenicum Concilium Vaticanum II: Constitutiones, Decreta, Declarationes*, Vatican, Libreria Editrice Vaticana, 1993, translated in Flannery, A. (ed.), as *Declaration on the Relation of the Church to Non-Christian Religions* in *Vatican Council II: The Conciliar and Post Conciliar Documents*, Michigan, Eerdmans, 1992.

15 See the remarks of George, Cardinal F., *How Liberalism Fails the Church*, in *Commonweal*, November 19, 1999, Vol. 126, No. 20.

16 Steinfels, P. *Reinventing Liberal Catholicism* in *Commonweal*, November 19, 1999, Vol. 126, No. 20.

unexamined, while theologians as a group are less inclined to engage in trenchant critique of one another's thought, and Catholic academics are all too easily diverted from self-criticism by a continuing preoccupation with the potential (or actual) threat of church authority.

# PART II
# THE PROGRAMME
# OF RADICAL ORTHODOXY

Chapter Three

# The Programme of Radical Orthodoxy

John Milbank

I have encountered a strange contrast in reactions to Radical Orthodoxy on opposite sides of the Atlantic. In Britain it seems to be regarded as an extreme, frightening movement. In North America, especially amongst Catholics, it is seen rather as a typically Anglican attempt at mediation. Most manifest in the American context seems to be the fact that it is neither decisively Roman Catholic nor Protestant, that it refuses both an emphatic Barthianism or any foundational natural theology, resisting either pure faith or pure reason, while it appeals once again to the Fathers as theological exemplars, and to Plato as the philosophical foreshadowing of revelation.

Now both these perceptions are true. Radical Orthodoxy is, indeed, a movement of intellectual, ecumenical and cultural mediation. It protests equally against assertions of pure reason and of pure faith; equally against denominational claims for a monopoly of salvation and against indifference to church order; equally against theology as an internal autistic idiolect, and against theology as an adaptation to unquestioned secular assumptions. In these senses it is a *via media*. However, it further asserts that the apparently opposite poles refused are in secret collusion: more specifically it contends that the pursuit of pure faith is as much a *modern* quest as the pursuit of pure reason; that the investing of salvific security entirely in institutions and formulae is as modern as the individualistic neglect of such matters, while the eschewing of all apologetics is likewise as modern as regarding apologetics as the essential foundation for a truthful theology. Hence Radical Orthodoxy's apparent moderation in distancing itself from the *soi-disant* 'conservatism' of revelatory positivism, or a high papalism, or a purely self-referential theological discourse, is actually a sign of an 'extremism' which removes itself from modernity in either its liberal or conservative guises.

Perhaps the most crucial instance of this simultaneous moderation and extremism can be seen in Radical Orthodoxy's stance towards Protestant neo-orthodoxy. In a sense it appears comparatively moderate by stressing more than the latter that all human reason is a participation in the divine mind and in allowing an essential role for divine manifestness in human experience. Yet more fundamentally, Radical Orthodoxy considers that Barthianism, as much as Natural Theology, is operating in a specifically modern space. Thus Barth inherits from certain currents of Nineteenth Century Protestant liberalism a Christological *riposte* to Kant's philosophy: since it is now supposed to be impossible for human reason to ascend beyond its limits to God, the only possible theology must be one exclusively grounded in the absolute divine descent of incarnation regarded more as a remedy for our finitude than our fallenness.

In this fashion Barth tends to embrace the post-Enlightenment notion of fixed ascertainable limit to human reason, and also, at times, the idea of a valid secular autonomy within those limits. The assertion of pure faith, pure unanticipated revelation over against reason, is the counterpart of an acceptance of an entirely secure but limited human reason, sovereign within its own terms of reference. By contrast, Radical Orthodoxy, re-invoking pre-modern positions (which already began to fade in the late Middle Ages), does not consider there to be any secure reason without reference to our remote and uncertain vision of the divine – an anticipation of the beatific vision granted by grace, which in a fallen world must take the shape of a figurative anticipation of the incarnate logos, or else, *anno Domini*, a commentary on the textual and sacramental relics of that incarnation. For this outlook, faith is not alien to reason, but simply its intensification. And if reason is already Christological, then inversely, faith, until the eschaton, remains dispersed in all the different discourses of human reason. To speak about God it must speak about something else; indeed its speaking about God really is only the difference it makes to speaking about something else.

This is what we mean by saying that, while compared to neo-orthodoxy, Radical Orthodoxy is less accommodating, since it allows for no entirely autonomous realms of secular discourse (even where these do not directly concern God or redemption), it is also more mediating, as it does not limit theology to a pure exegetical exposition of the word of God according to its own absolutely discrete logic. Or rather, one could say, the discreteness of theology lies not *only* in the Christocentric *forma* but also in the constantly new pneumatalogical performances of this *forma* by an enhanced reason in interaction with manifold human life-forms and thought-forms. (It should be added here that this stance toward Barth leaves open the question of our attitude towards the first reformers, especially Luther, since sometimes they can be read as at least half-recuperating forgotten aspects of Patristic and high Mediæval thought.)

This situation of Radical Orthodoxy with respect to twentieth century Protestant thought is complemented by its situation with respect to Roman Catholic thought in the same period. Here the alliance to the *nouvelle théologie* is stronger than that to neo-orthodoxy. Radical Orthodoxy considers that Henri de Lubac was a greater theological revolutionary than Karl Barth, because in questioning a hierarchical duality of grace and nature as discrete stages, he transcended, unlike Barth, the shared background assumption of all modern theology. In this way one could say, anachronistically, that he inaugurated a postmodern theology. The radical implication of de Lubac's work (which he himself had to hedge round with immense caution) is that, for Aquinas and the preceding tradition, faith and reason are not essentially distinct, since both are but differing degrees of participation in the mind of God.

In the case of Aquinas, for reason to be reason, it must aspire to the complete knowledge of the beatific vision, yet such aspiration, as exceeding finite nature, must somehow receive some dim glimpse of that vision in advance if it is to recognise it even as a possibility. Reason ascending, therefore, is an inchoate and relatively non-discursive anticipation of the final end, and in consequence reason ascending is already grace descending. And just as both reason and faith are framed by the participation of our being and knowing in the divine being and intellection, so also they are both – reason as much as faith – framed by eschatology. For reason to think at all, it must somehow already know what it seeks to know: reason, to be reason, must therefore also be faith, and in articulating this view in different ways Augustine, Anselm and Aquinas are all conscious that at the heart of their Christian articulation of grace and revelation they are nonetheless radicalising and resolving the specifically Platonic view that reason, to be reason, in some fashion knows before it knows. Thus in reflecting upon scripture, they do not depart from, but intensify, dialectical reflection – although, beyond dialectics, its aporias are resolved through the notion that divine descent allows our ascent by coming to meet us in the materiality of sensory encounter and liturgical offering.[1]

If, however, Radical Orthodoxy perpetuates the *nouvelle théologie*, why give it a glossy new name? There are three good reasons for this. First, Radical Orthodoxy, if catholic, is not a specifically Roman Catholic theology; although it can be espoused by Roman Catholics, it can equally be espoused by those who are formally 'protestant', yet whose theory and practice essentially accords with the catholic vision of the Patristic period through to the high Middle Ages. Second, Roman Catholic theology actually finds it hugely difficult to come to terms with de Lubac's legacy. This legacy incurs the suspicion of liberals for not allowing a common human rational discourse and foundation for theology, and of conservatives for much the same reasons, allied to a fear of relativism and diminution of church influence. Thus the implications of any re-reading of Aquinas on grace and nature, and on faith and reason, for the non-autonomy of philosophy, ethics, and politics, have still not been entirely thought through (the encyclical letter *Fides et Ratio* is ambivalent here, although at times it seems to come close to a Radically Orthodox perspective). Third, and most controversially, in certain ways Roman Catholicism can be seen (though clearly could be so seen without contradiction by Roman Catholics themselves) as profoundly colluding with a modernity it helped to construct.

Ever since the Gregorian reforms, the Roman Catholic church has arguably over-insisted on clerical control of a specifically 'spiritual' social space, which (as Charles Péguy argued) has left the laity, disenfranchised as Christians, with nothing left to do but invent their own sphere of securely 'secular' operations. To be sure, Anglicanism usually has made the opposite and equally modern error of ultimate control of ecclesial institutions by power organised for secular ends. Nonetheless at times and in places it has preserved a certain blurring of boundaries congenial to Radical Orthodoxy – an Anglican fuzziness which is apparently moderate, but secretly extreme.

It is this blurring, this non-duality of reason and faith, secular and social, which I want to emphasise, because it has often been misunderstood. Radical Orthodoxy favours no theocracy, because theocracy is predicated upon the very dualism it rejects: for the sacred hierophants to be enthroned there must

---

1  On this see further Catherine Pickstock's article in this volume and for the above view of Aquinas my article *Intensities* in *Modern Theology*, October 1999, Vol. XV, No. 4.

be a drained secular space for them to command. But for Radical Orthodoxy there is no such space. For Radical Orthodoxy, the sacral interpenetrates everywhere, and if it descends from above, this descent is also manifest through its rising up from below. Thus to say there is only the sacred is equally to say that, for now, within the *sæculum*, there is only the secular, which is nonetheless only human time through its sacral intimations. And such intimations are dispersed in complex social and cultural patterns of tradition and spontaneity – not secured in positive absolute sources of authority standing over against humanity.

The foregoing, is, I think, relevant to the charge that Radical Orthodoxy cannot be catholic, as it tends to denigrate the role and integrity of an independent reason. I would contend that the advocacy of such a reason is *not* truly catholic, but the outcome of late Mediæval and Baroque deviations. However, this is not to say that we simply oppose all apologetic. Indeed, subtle critics of Radical Orthodoxy argue that it is *too* liberal and apologetic, as it tends to start with some non-specifically Christian category such as peace, gift, liturgy, motion, beauty, or whatever – and then argue that only Christian thought and practice safeguards the purity of this category. It is as though (as Michael Banner wittily puts it) it were a secular princess requiring rescue by a Christian Knight. However, here once again, the idea of an absolutely internal Christian discourse is really the reactive counter to the notion of apologetics based upon a neutral starting point. For if, indeed, there are no 'general' notions uncontaminated by the contingencies of language and circumstance, then equally there is no pure concrete given starting point uncontaminated by general abstract notions. Thus the concreteness of the gospels is also a mosaic of inherited general and vague notions and images, and there is no sheerly Christian language which will not be somewhat understood by non-Christians.

In consequence the Fathers and early- to high-Scholastics made little sharp division between exposition of the faith upon the basis of its own supra-rational assumptions, and discursive developments of this faith that are to a degree convincing even to those outside faith's circle. Thus I, at least, do not apologise for residual apologetics, as it is the questionable duality of internal discourse versus *apologia* which I seek to surpass.

So far I have indicated the situation of Radical Orthodoxy with respect to Protestant and Catholic thought. I would like to add some remarks about its relation to recent British theology, to postmodernism, and to the contemporary theological scene in general.

First, let me discuss the situation of recent English theology. Most of the British people involved in Radical Orthodoxy are to a degree heirs to the peculiarly British refraction of neo-orthodoxy represented by Donald MacKinnon, who, in effect, sought to develop something like a more philosophically self-conscious Barthianism in which its Kantian presuppositions were much more specifically brought to the fore. There was, indeed, a certain blurring of boundaries involved here, and also a peculiar style of inter-disciplinary *collage* far removed from any exegetical straitjacket. It seems to me that Radical Orthodoxy has to acknowledge its indebtedness as to *idiom* to this MacKinnon-derived legacy. But as to content it is equally important to stress a break with MacKinnon and some of his assumptions.

At this point, especially, I can only give certain sketchy indications which illustrate what I mean in the space available. Primarily, Radical Orthodoxy does not situate itself in a post-Kantian intellectual space which tends to identify a correct insistence on the *finitude* of our knowledge with the false idea that we can once and for all specify the bounds of possible knowledge for finite minds. Here one should not embrace a story commonly accepted (by the Transcendental Thomists, and others) according to which Kant may be reconciled with Patristic and high Mediæval tradition, because his rejection of speculative metaphysics is a refusal of a late-Scholastic distortion of the tradition, falsely claiming that we enjoy a special intellectual intuition of the first cause as Being as such. Rather, one should embrace an alternative story based upon more recent and more exact research, which instead narrates how Kant is the *fulfilment*, not the overturning, of late Scholasticism.

Roughly speaking this story goes as follows. An ontology entirely prior to theology and unaffected by an orientation to revelation, which emerged in early modernity, depended upon the post-Scotist notion that one can univocally grasp Being as indifferent to infinite and finite. This allowed one to think of infinite Being as simply *a* being, which either exists or does not exist, in the same fashion as any finite creature. Hence Being had here ceased to be a perfective term subject to more or less. And once God had ceased to surmount, through consummate transcendence, this perfective scale and is instead regarded as a mere supreme item, he soon gets thought of as first cause in univocally the same sense as later finite causes, and then eventually as self-caused, as the supreme self-determining will laying down arbitrary laws and so forth, as with Descartes. To this quasi-physical god it was supposed to be possible to make a natural theological ascent in an apodeictic mode based upon pure reason. However, once Being is seen as lacking in any depth of intrinsic perfection, but rather as clearly apparent – or at least inferable as either there or not – then already Being is defined in terms of knowledge, rather than vice versa. Thus the very first pure metaphysics, free of an extra-rational practice of erotic ascent (as with Plato), or of the reception of sacramental grace (as with Christianity) – in other words the first pure ontology delivered by reason alone which emerged in the early seventeenth century – was *already* better to be expressed as a fundamental epistemology. This transition quickly began to take place, and Kant only completes an internal movement already half-undergone by Baroque Scholasticism itself. Moreover, he also completes, and does not finally abandon, its project of natural theology.

For Kant, the finite being of appearances is pre-determined by the possibilities given in the framework of our mediated knowing of this being, while the infinite Being of real, spiritual, noumenal, existence, is pre-determined through the purest self-realising possibility of spiritual existence or reason as such; and as rational beings we can univocally grasp this possibility. Thus the 'ought' implying the 'can' of practical reason, which further implies an actual moral order of possible goodness and judgement, affirms practically (and really also theoretically, since for Kant practical reason is a purer theory) the ontological argument only denied when it was a matter of schematising reason in terms of the contingency of appearances and not the pure self-realising possibility of reason in its noumenal purity. Kant *perfects* metaphysical dogmatism because his limiting of the import of the phenomenal is only attained by a safeguarding of the noumenal against the phenomenal, which after all is the real pietistic, anti-Catholic and anti 'mystical' aim of the critical philosophy. What is refused here is not groundless extrapolation from the phenomenal, but rather (without grounds) any notion of attributive analogy or participation, that is to say any real kinship between the visible and the invisible worlds (as has been well argued by Phillip Blond).[2]

---

2  See the *Introduction* to Blond, P. (ed.), *Post-Secular Philosophy*, London, Routledge, 1998.

If one fails to realise this, then the danger is that one will confuse the Kantian sublimity of pure infinite possibility with the traditional theological notion of a divine darkness that is not the abyss of contentless will, but rather the darkness to us of an utterly dazzling light suffusing its manifold infinite of *formed* content with the full intensity of a single illumination. Out of this confusion one gets the doubtful piety of a transcendentalist apophaticism investing claims to an absolute unknowing with the self-righteous holiness of supposed superior reserve. Where, in this mentality, as Hegel rightly demanded, is the God for whose sake one risks action and affirmation? Where is the God who makes any difference?

Closely allied to this misunderstood *via negativa* goes a false subscription to the illusion that moral and intellectual 'depth' pertains to the notion of the tragic. This involves some flirtation with the idea that there are absolute limits to ethical response – not as one must freely admit (and indeed insist) in this or that situation for this or that individual – but absolutely and collectively and across time. Obviously the danger here is that one implicitly posits some kind of positive content to evil, and so, in Manichæan fashion, a power outside the Divine. Usually, proponents of a tragic theology make great play of sophisticated resistance to speculative closure. But quite manifestly – for the Greeks as well as for Hegel – tragedy (especially) is speculative closure. In the Greek case, tragedy records the 'end of history' in the founding of the *polis*: here primitive sacrifice and primitive impulse to revenge is once and for all limited, and yet allowed a certain continued sway, since it is recruited as an essential aspect of civic *nomos*. Here, instead of striving entirely to overcome violence and seeming inescapable quandary, or at least hoping for such an overcoming, one instead compromises with violence and dilemma and then hypostasises this compromise as inevitable.

This precisely *is* speculative closure in time which absolutises finite perplexity and apparent scarcity and so *usurps* the beatific vision.[3] A certain pietistic focus upon Good Friday, reluctant even to anticipate a Resurrection rejoicing (though for sure, prior to the eschaton, we may not altogether abandon ourselves to it) as though this would be somewhat unrefined, therefore still executes what it most abhors, namely a theodicy substituting for hope and practice. In like manner it still, contrary to its imaginings, celebrates a Hegelian *speculative* Good Friday, which offers up to a pagan divinity

---

3   I am indebted here to discussions with David Hart of the University of Virginia.

human sufferings in time which are never to be physically redeemed. In this understanding it is thought that one refuses the banal idea that future redemption will justify past suffering, especially that of innocents and of children. And yet instead what one arrives at is the much more horrifying notion of a never-released present moment (as exemplified by Ivan Karamazov's locked-up child) somehow in sacred communion with its eternal yield of a fruitless depth of eternal commiseration never communicated to the one suffering. By contrast one should see that Ivan Karamazov's mistake is to *spatialise* suffering, and so not to see that there is *no* moment of itself which is eternal, no moment which cannot be broken into by the memory of security, or the later narrative location within a story of liberation. Since there is no 'punctual' eternal present, there never has been and never will be any child absolutely and forever confined. And once unconfined, it *never was* absolutely confined, because the mere appearance of such confinement is simply the way the finitude of time can be distorted by the privative motion of evil (always contingent and never tragically necessitated) into the apparent spatial self-sufficiency of an immanent moment.

The liberating hand of the good restores, retrospectively (and *really*), even this seemingly 'captive' moment back to the mould of the true finite which passes as an opening into the infinite. In this way a biographically narrated redemption of past suffering, which can also be that of a collective subject (but not, and never, as it is with Hegel, of the unredeemed passions of *some* for the future salvation of *others*), need not after all be banal, and indeed, this alone prevents the banality (lurking within illusory depths) of the tragic vision. (It should be stressed here that the critique of Hegel implied by these remarks need not preclude sympathy with many other aspects of Hegel's endeavour.)

The strange thing about all this post-Kantian and post-Hegelian hypostasising of the negative and the tragic is that it is actually *highly* postmodern in character, or at least incipiently so – much more than Radical Orthodoxy. This is because it sets up a lack of mediation between the infinite and unknown on the one hand and the finite and known on the other. For if the finite and known mediates to us nothing of the infinite, then ultimately the very truth of the finite is suspended and relativised. The only advantage of the specifically postmodern over this 'modern' legacy is that it more or less comes clean about its anti-humanism and nihilism. To begin with, back in the 1980's, I certainly saw postmodernism as a moment of opportunity for theology, because it seemed to qualify and diminish secular claims to truth. At the same time, I considered that its claimed exposure of the arbitrary assumptions of all discourses *itself* made the assumption of an ultimate ontological violence, an assumption which might be relativised in turn by theology (though by theology alone). The latter, I considered, might be regarded as the discourse making a wager on the possible harmony of all discourses in a universe that might be harmonised, since it rested on an ultimate harmonious source, now obscured. I noted the unfounded character of the nihilist demonstration of the truth of untruth, or of an endless shuttle between the really true void that is nothing on the one hand, and appearances which, if untrue, are again nothing on the other, amounting to a kind of hypostasised law of the non-identity of nothing.

I thought that, with equal plausibility, theology might once again, as with Plato and Augustine, assert the reality of truth. This assertion could be made only by affirming an unchanging and simple eternity, in which temporal flux remotely and confusingly participates, yet nonetheless partially shows, so saving its own appearance. Whereas for nihilism the void is not, and therefore time is not either (as Catherine Pickstock explains in her essay in this volume), for theology eternity is, and therefore time and the body also are. Theology, in consequence, could claim not only to save matter, but to be the only possible materialism.

This legacy – summed up as 'suspending the material' – has now been taken up into Radical Orthodoxy (and it is, one should note, allied to unrepentant, but not priggishly uncritical, left-wing political commitments). However, I now see that nihilism is not something newly advanced by the postmodern after Nietzsche; to the contrary, it is inherent in the modern – in Kant and Hegel themselves. More specifically it is latent in the Kantian sublime, and in the Hegelian view that the absolute as nothing *is* through its self-alienation as the finite, and its equally necessary – again to preserve itself as absolute – negation of this finite. This negation of the negation leaves the finite in its contingency or arbitrary 'untruth', as nonetheless the truth of the absolute. Increasingly scholars are recognising Hegel's self-confessed nihilism and the same monotonous conceptual pattern of shuttle between the nothing of the void or flux and the nothing of apparent contingent 'presence' traceable from idealism to Heidegger, and via Russian nihilism and Kojève to the French generation of the 1960's. And in this light, appeals to (Kantian or

Hegelian) humanism against the postmodernists look increasingly desperate. The reverse face of humanism itself has usually been an impersonal immanentism and a gospel of cosmic futility.

The theological turn against nihilism is common ground between Radical Orthodoxy and French Catholic phenomenologists-cum-theologians like Jean-Luc Marion. But here again Radical Orthodoxy in one sense seeks to mediate – and this time between French phenomenology on the one hand, and an Anglo-Saxon focus on language on the other. For the Anglo-Saxon linguistic obsession, whether Wittgensteinian or Derridean (Derrida has been overwhelmingly most successful in English speaking countries), the stress is that we are inevitably located inside words, conventions, and traditions. Sometimes the danger here is of textualising aridity, of formality and smug self-reference. Moreover, a notion that we are 'trapped' inside language can re-affirm transcendentalist knowable limits to finitude, and in consequence, encourage an over-agnostic construal of analogical discourse about God.

Phenomenology, by contrast, insists on the novelty of vision, of irreducible encounter. But the idea of an 'original intuition' ignores linguistic, cultural, and historical mediation. It is irredeemably apolitical. And if, in this way, one ignores the reception of experience by *judgement*, then one will forget that in recognising the relation of the unknown to the known one is judging this relation. In forgetfulness of such a judgement one may imagine that there is a raw intuition of the unknown and its relation to the known, which can only take the form of hypostasising that very unknownness and invisibility, as precisely that which one encounters. Thus, curiously enough, phenomenological theology also tends to conclude that there is a lack of a mediation between finite and infinite – emphasising 'distance' rather than participation – and again with an over-agnostic construal of analogy.

By contrast, for a mediating perspective, linguistic expression and intuitive experience are inseparable. We see in making, make in seeing, and this constitutes one main point of Catherine Pickstock's liturgical turn.[4] Since God is not an item in the world to which we might turn, he is only first there for us in our turning to him. And yet we only turn to him when he reaches us; herein lies the mystery of liturgy – liturgy which for theology is more fundamental than *either* language *or* experience, and yet is both linguistic and experiential.

4  Pickstock, C., *After Writing: On The Liturgical Consummation of Philosophy*, Oxford, Blackwell, 1998.

However, in mediating between phenomenology and linguistic philosophy, Radical Orthodoxy is also more extreme than both, since both collude in losing what they claim to preserve – namely language and intuitive experience. A relativist linguistic philosophy loses language, because to say that language shows nothing beyond language is to exit language by establishing transcendentalist bounds for it. By contrast, the theological view that language *of itself* manifests (but not by looking outside language) remains within language, since it is no transcendentalist claim, but rather is made only in relation to certain privileged linguistic or symbolic forms deemed to be especially disclosive. Furthermore, if language of itself discloses, one may validly suppose ultimate reality to be hyper-linguistic, and not a void beyond *logos*.

Equally if, for phenomenology, all one sees of the unknown is its invisibility, then one loses visibility, and any foretaste, for now, of beatitude. But paradoxically, where one allows vision to be contaminated by judgement – and also desire – then one may judge, yearningly, that the invisible is shown in the visible, and so save ultimate visibility.

Radical Orthodoxy is, therefore, in this case also more extreme than the alternatives it mediates, in that it strives beyond arbitrarily imagined limits both to see and to speak, both to speak and to see.

If, as we have seen, Radical Orthodoxy seeks to mediate between opposed movements in our time, is this undertaken *entirely* in the name of its extreme opposition to modernity? Is its radicalism only that of a returning to roots? Not entirely, and not only. It is also a radicalism which regards orthodoxy, in theory and practice, as a project always to be completed, and certainly not as perfected within pre-modernity. I have already mentioned how, for Radical Orthodoxy, the time of error is really the decadence of Catholic Christendom itself in the late Middle Ages, such that the specifically 'modern' in the Reformation, and also, I might now add, in the Enlightenment, often displays a correct critique of such decadence.

This holds good even if, at a deeper level, the modern sustains the late Mediæval: for example, in the Enlightenment's rejection of an arbitrary God, and arbitrary ecclesial rule according to formalistic norms, itself issues in the promotion of natural and human arbitrariness, resulting in a purer formalism supposedly devoid of mystique. However, in a more positive fashion, modernity has often extended the drive towards liberty, equality, fraternity, individual expressiveness, romantic love, historicity, and the celebration of the spatially- and temporally-bound ordinary and local, all of which were indeed already manifest in the early to high Middle Ages, and yet not sufficiently released.[5]

The problem, however, with the modern 'release' of these ideals, as with the modern release of materialism alluded to earlier, is that in gradually losing their theological and teleological ground, their character as ideals becomes distorted, and, in consequence, eventually cease to be credible. Freedom becomes freedom without point, freedom for futility; equality, without a basis in the common good (as a measure for sharing according to capacity and assigned role) degenerates into a treatment of all people formally as the same – a treatment that both disguises and constitutes actual brutal disparities. Fraternity is likewise soon corroded by the suspicion of a more fundamental egotism, seen as often hidden under the mask of projection, such that one ceases to believe in the irreducible mystery of an ontologically grounded elective affinity. Meanwhile creativity that expresses no transcendental beauty is only demonstrable as the force of sublime shock, whilst romantic love outside of a trust in affinity and the capacity of beauty to disclose truth sinks into fictional sentiment, alternating with a raw drive to dominate the other. Equally, concrete localities which no longer enshrine the transcendent must either be denied in the name of the abstract or universal, or else be violently insisted upon at the expense of other identities (or else both tendencies are somehow fearfully combined).

Finally, where it is perceived that all is involved in pointless change, it is also perceived that nothing really changes. What remains is power – not even will, but an anonymous power that we are driven by, and whose recognition by us exposes all the ideals of modernity discussed earlier as fond illusions. Only the theological can restore these ideals by re-shaping them. Hence Radical Orthodoxy, although it opposes the modern, also seeks to save it. It espouses, not the pre-modern, but an alternative version of modernity.

---

5  In insisting on the Mediæval origins of these things, I hold unashamedly to the main traditions of British historiography, as exemplified, for example, by Stubbs and Maitland, as opposed to *some* continental tendencies to erect myths of absolute 'breaks' with an over-generalised *ancien régime*.

Chapter Four

# A Catholic Response to
# the Programme of Radical Orthodoxy

Fergus Kerr OP

## I

To provide, however provisionally and only to inaugurate discussion, 'a (Roman) Catholic response' to Radical Orthodoxy, as I have been asked to do, might seem quite easy. The book, *Radical Orthodoxy*, is the principal manifestation, even 'manifesto', of the 'movement'. Given that the three editors, John Milbank, Catherine Pickstock, and Graham Ward, are all members of the Church of England, it might look like an Anglican phenomenon, straightforward enough for an outsider to discuss.

The book itself is widely perceived, in the no doubt somewhat restricted circle in which these esoteric matters are noticed at all, as initiating a movement comparable with (say) the interests of the group around *Lux Mundi*, the collection of essays published in 1889 by a group of Anglican scholars in Oxford under the editorship of Charles Gore,[1] the intention of which was 'to put the Catholic faith into its right relation to modern intellectual and moral problems'. It turns out, however, as we learn on the *Acknowledgements* page of *Radical Orthodoxy*, that, though the three editors and seven of the twelve contributors are Anglicans, "all of a High Church persuasion", the other five contributors are actually Roman Catholics. What I have to say could, of course, in any case, only be *one* Catholic response. As we shall see, there might well be radically different ones; but, given the number of Catholic contributors to the book, *Radical Orthodoxy*, it is not possible for *any* Catholic response to come from a wholly external standpoint. Catholics of a Roman persuasion, so to speak, are already inside the project as participants.

---

1   Gore, C. (ed.), *Lux Mundi: a Series of Studies in the Religion of the Incarnation*, London, John Murray, 1889.

This is not simply a High Anglican project. As we shall see, the project is easy enough to locate, historically and textually, in terms of a controversy internal to Roman Catholic theology throughout most of the twentieth century.

It is, however, "very much a Cambridge collection", as the *Acknowledgements* page tells us.[2] The Cambridge figures who are invoked as 'influences' are as follows: Donald MacKinnon, Rowan Williams, Nicholas Lash, David Ford, Janet Martin Soskice, Tim Jenkins and Lewis Ayres. Influences from outside Cambridge are also named: Stanley Hauerwas, Professor of Ethics at Duke University and soon to give Gifford lectures at the University of St Andrews; David Burrell of Notre Dame who has written widely on Thomas Aquinas; the Jesuits, Michael Buckley, whose book *At the Origins of Modern Atheism*[3] is a key text in the grand narrative of the failure of Enlightenment theology; and Walter J Ong, the first to draw attention to the baneful influence of Peter Ramus' logic in Paris in the 1520's on the eve of the Reformation;[4] as well as Gillian Rose, whose *The Broken Middle*,[5] written before she became a Christian, and interweaves Milbank's book *Theology and Social Theory: Beyond Secular Reason* (the *magnum opus* at the back of the Radical Orthodoxy project) in her own formidable and startlingly original rejection of what she sees as the spurious opposition of post-modernity to the Western metaphysical tradition.[6] While noting that these figures who have influenced the volume 'would sympathise with much, but often not all of it' (and, in some cases, surely, often not much of it!), this array of names certainly inserts Radical Orthodoxy into one of the most productive and distinctive networks within Anglo-American theology today.

## II

It is not difficult to identify other groupings in Britain with quite different sets of interests, who might find *Radical Orthodoxy* profoundly alien and

---

2   *Radical Orthodoxy*, p. xi.

3   Buckley, M., *At the Origins of Modern Atheism*, New Haven, Yale University Press, 1987.

4   Ong, W., *Ramus, Method, and the Decay of Dialogue*, Massachusetts, Harvard University Press, 1958.

5   Rose, G., *The Broken Middle : Out of Our Ancient Society*, Oxford, Blackwell, 1992.

6   Milbank, J., *Theology and Social Theory: Beyond Secular Reason*, Oxford, Blackwell, 1990.

uncongenial. For example, the *Forum for Religion and Theology* convened by Ian Markham and Gareth Jones at Liverpool Hope University in 1997 has issued a manifesto about the state of theology in Britain (in England, effectively), which repeats the central concerns of 'liberal Protestantism', noting that "a plurality of approaches in theological method and formulation needs to be encouraged" for "a time of undeniable change".[7] Signed by thirty-four theologians, including a handful of Roman Catholics, this document explicitly hopes for the creation, in due course, of "a British equivalent to the American Academy of Religion". Their opening admission that there are "problems involved with traditional liberal theology" suggests that they may have been reading Milbank ("it linked itself too uncritically with individualism and progress ... its greatest failure was not to appreciate the richness of the Christian tradition, a tradition which was too often caricatured and misunderstood"). Their references to 'conservative theologies' might suggest that some of them would regard Radical Orthodoxy much as they no doubt regard Karl Barth's neo-orthodox Calvinism or Hans Urs von Balthasar's Catholicism.

Then again, if Colin Gunton's very hostile editorial in the second issue of *The International Journal of Systematic Theology* is anything to go by, King's College London may harbour adversaries of Radical Orthodoxy who belong to a classically Reformed and Calvinist school, and regard what they would see as Radical Orthodoxy's melange of patristic theology and postmodern philosophy with distaste and alarm. Gunton's distaste leads him to conclude "it must be said that public claims to orthodoxy such as this run the risk of calling attention not to the Lord and his Christ but to the rightness of the believer or the group".[8]

No one interested in Christian theology can look round the contemporary scene without being delighted by the amount of vigorous argument, and even awed by the vitality of *odium theologicum*. However marginal Christian religion may have become in Western, and certainly in British, society, measured at any rate by the decline in church attendance, the last decade has revealed a good deal of passionate interest still, in academic circles, in Christian theology.

---

7  *Reviews in Religion and Theology*, 1998, No. 2, pp. 11-13.
8  Gunton, C. *Editorial* in *The International Journal of Systematic Theology*, July 1999, Vol. 1, No. 2, p. 117.

## III

The most provocative remark in the *Acknowledgements*, no doubt, is the 'resonance with the Cambridge past' which the contributors hope to hear in the frequent appeal throughout the essays to Plato, Augustine, Anselm, and Aquinas, as well as to 'the spirit of Ralph Cudworth and Christopher Smart'.

Ralph Cudworth (1617-88), it may be recalled, was the central figure among the Anglicans usually described as 'the Cambridge Platonists'. In his principal work, *The True Intellectual System of the Universe*, first published in 1678,[9] he contends, against the Hobbesian atheism of the day, that the only real source of knowledge is Christian revelation. In a way, that might seem not too unlike the principal contention of Milbank's *Theology and Social Theory*.

Christopher Smart (1722-71), a much more provocative (even tongue-in-cheek?) invocation, is no doubt best known for one poem ("For I will consider my Cat Jeffrey").[10] He was entered at Pembroke College Cambridge in 1739 and despite spending most of his time in taverns and running up debts, he became fellow of the college, Prælector in philosophy, and keeper of the common chest in 1745. He developed what was regarded as religious mania and was confined in an asylum for two years (1756-58), at which time he was visited by Dr Samuel Johnson who (famously) thought him quite sane (and was memorialised in verse: 'Let Johnson, House of Johnson, rejoice with/ Omphalocarpa a type of bur, God be gracious to Samuel Johnson'). 'A Song of David', written in the asylum, often compared with Blake's visionary poems, was printed in 1763, excluded from the collection posthumously issued in 1791, reprinted in 1819 and has had a chequered history since, often in abridged versions. Like most of his poetry, it is liturgical and even (one may say) doxological in character ('For ADORATION all the ranks/ Of angels yield eternal thanks/ And David in the midst/ With God's good poor, which, last and least/ In man's esteem, thou to thy feast/ O blessed bride-groom, bidst').

9    Cudworth, R, *The True Intellectual System of the Universe*, London, Walthoe *et el.* 1743.
10   Callan, N. (ed.), *The Collected Poems of Christopher Smart*, London Routledge and Kegan Paul, 1949, Vol. I, *Iubilate Agno*, p. 249 ff., (XIX, p. 311).

While Christopher Smart is not cited anywhere in the book, his spirit may surely be allowed to hover over a collection that concludes with essays on aesthetics (by Frederick Christian Bauerschmidt), painting (Phillip Blond) and Augustine's *de Musica* (Catherine Pickstock), testifying to the way in which *Radical Orthodoxy* represents a theological project with strongly poetic and liturgical dimensions. After all, in Catherine Pickstock's book *After Writing* the principal theme is that language, instead of being a way of representing reality, is, because it is radically *doxological*, a way of praising God.[11]

Plato, Augustine, Anselm, and Aquinas, are more conventional authorities to invoke – yet of course already very contestable, by current academic theological criteria. In many – perhaps most – universities these days it is unlikely that students of theology would spend much time engaged with such authors. It is, for instance, as the syllabus would confirm, perfectly possible to gain a degree in Christian theology at the University of Oxford without encountering any of them. The compulsory examination papers which frame the curriculum take the student through Scripture to 451 AD and then allow him or her to leap a millennium to settle on post-Enlightenment developments such as the history of Christology from Kant to Troeltsch. Elsewhere, and more generally, if Augustine is read at all, it is as the source of almost every disaster in Western civilisation, let alone in Christian theology. Radical Orthodoxy, on the other hand, largely ignores the Reformation and deplores most of what has happened in theology since the Enlightenment.

## IV

There are two centrally important discussions of Luther in *Radical Orthodoxy*. The first, by John Montag, explores the highly influential though little studied work of Francisco Suárez.[12] He shows that for Thomas Aquinas (as opposed to Suárez) revelation was never anything that happened on its own before becoming part of human thought and judgement. This has the consequence of demonstrating that Aquinas already held what Luther sought later to recover: namely, that what God reveals is also an intimate self manifestation,

---

11 Pickstock, C., *After Writing: The Liturgical Consummation of Philosophy*, Oxford, Blackwell, 1997.

12 Montag, J., *Revelation: The False Legacy of Suárez* in *Radical Orthodoxy*, p. 57.

the word that pours from the heart and animates faith: precisely the dimension Luther insisted on.

The second is John Milbank's own attempt to renew theological interest in Lutheran thinkers like Hamann and Jacobi.[13] Here we read that Luther himself never escaped the 'post-Scotist legacy': provocatively, we are assured that he entertained no such project as 'knowledge by faith alone'. Indeed, Milbank adds: "on the contrary, [Luther] broadly accepted the framework of late Mediæval nominalist philosophy". Far from having escaped from the shackles of that 'whore Reason', Luther would have remained imprisoned in the most decadent kind of late-Mediæval metaphysics.

In what seems to me a key passage for understanding the entire Radical Orthodoxy project, Milbank goes on as follows:

> This philosophy was itself the legatee of the greatest of all disruptions carried out in the history of European thought, namely that of Duns Scotus, who for *the first time* established a radical separation of philosophy from theology by declaring that it was possible to consider being in abstraction from the question of whether one is considering created or creating being. Eventually this generated the notion of an ontology and an epistemology unconstrained by, and transcendentally prior to, theology itself. In the late Middle Ages and in early modernity, philosophy became essentially the pursuit of such an ontology and epistemology, and the Reformation did nothing to disturb this situation.[14]

Here, to back that claim, Milbank refers us to works by J.-F. Courtine, Eric Alliez and Michel de Certeau.[15] Milbank continues:

> Indeed the Reformation was itself predetermined by it, in that once philosophy has arrogated to itself the knowledge of Being as such, theology starts to become a regional, ontic, positive science, grounded either upon certain revealed facts or upon grace-given inner dispositions or again upon external present authority (the Counter Reformation model).[16]

---

13 Milbank, J., *Knowledge: The Theological Critique of Philosophy in Hamann and Jacobi* in *Radical Orthodoxy*, pp. 21-37.
14 Milbank, J., *Knowledge*, pp. 24; 23.
15 Milbank, J., *Knowledge*, p. 34, note 5.
16 Milbank, J., *Knowledge*, p. 24.

There would be much to debate here. Is this account of John Duns Scotus, roughly the same as Étienne Gilson's in *Being and Some Philosophers*,[17] confirmed by more conventional mediævalists than those whom Milbank cites? Is it true that Luther held no such doctrine as that knowledge of God is available only by faith in Christ, but was stuck in late Mediæval Nominalism? And so on. Every theological programme includes a reading of previous theological work, necessarily selective, and may thus be disputable at various points.

The really new thing, on Milbank's story, is the emergence of Protestantism and Tridentine Catholicism as a result of the radical split in late Mediæval thought between philosophy and theology – this new idea that Being may be considered independently of the doctrine of creation – that ontology and epistemology may be disengaged from theology. Thus emerges a way of doing philosophy apart from theology which would eventually lead to a philosophy without interest in the challenging questions of human destiny (afflicted by *Seinsvergessenheit* as Heidegger would say; settling for much too modest aims as John Paul II would say, in *Fides et Ratio*).[18] The Reformation itself, Milbank contends, was predetermined by this 'Scotist' claim that philosophy had access to knowledge of Being as such, independently of theology. Whatever the resulting fate of philosophy, Milbank's contention is clearly that once philosophy becomes independent of theology, theology loses its concern with reality as a whole. It fragments, grounding itself on certain 'revealed facts' (as perhaps the *Offenbarungspositivismus*, or positivism of revelation, with which critics have charged Barth's theology); or on certain 'grace-given inner dispositions' (Catholic modernism, liberal Protestantism, everything that George Lindbeck would call 'experiential-expressivism'[19]); or it grounds itself on 'external present authority' (as, for example, the living voice of the Magisterium, much as in Pope Pius XII's account of theology as merely explication of papal teaching).

In other words, when philosophy breaks free of theology, theology eventually, according to Milbank's typology here, becomes either Barthian

17  Gilson, É., *Being and Some Philosophers*, Toronto, Pontifical Institute of Mediæval Studies, 1952, pp. 85-94.

18  John Paul II, Encyclical Letter *Fides et Ratio*, Vatican, Libreria Editrice Vaticana, 1998. Translated as *Faith and Reason*, London, Catholic Truth Society, 1998.

19  Lindbeck, G. A., *The Nature of Doctrine : Religion and Theology in a Postliberal Age*, Philadelphia, Westminster Press, 1984, p. 16.

fideism, liberal-Protestant subjectivism, or ultramontane authoritarianism. Contrasting with that, in the patristic period with its reading of Scripture in the light of ancient philosophy, and right into early Mediæval Catholicism (both in theology and also in its sensibility), there was no opposition between reason and revelation. Milbank says:

> The very notion of a reason/revelation duality, far from being an authentic Christian legacy, itself results only from the rise of a questionable secular mode of knowledge. By contrast, in the Church Fathers or the early scholastics, both faith and reason are included in the more generic framework of participation in the mind of God: to reason truly one must be already illuminated by God, while revelation itself is but a higher measure of such illumination, conjoined intrinsically and inseparably with a created event which symbolically discloses that transcendent reality, to which all created events to a lesser degree also point.[20]

Here Milbank refers us to Avery Dulles, *The Assurance of Things Hoped For*, and an earlier book by René Latourelle.[21]


## V


There is much here that is deeply attractive to a Catholic like myself, reared in a certain French Thomist theology in the years before Vatican II took effect. With figures like Maritain in the background (especially the work *Three Reformers*),[22] we regarded what happened in Western Christianity in the sixteenth century as a complete disaster. *Radical Orthodoxy* fits very comfortably with that pre-Vatican II perspective; I share their delight and pleasure that, not just Thomas Aquinas but especially Augustine and the patristic tradition – in short, Christian neo-Platonism – are (under God) the things that make us happy to be Christians. Of course there are problems; we should not be interested in theology, philosophy or the very idea of orthodoxy,

---

20  Milbank, J., *Knowledge*, p. 24.
21  Milbank, J., *Knowledge*, p. 34, note 6. Dulles, A, *The Assurance of Things Hoped For: A Theology of Christian Faith*, New York, Clarendon Press, 1994; Latourelle, R., *Theology of Revelation*, New York, Fordham University Press, 1967.
22  Maritain, J., *Trois Réformateurs: Luther, Descartes, Rousseau (avec six portraits)*, Paris, Plon-Nourrit, 1925. Translated as *Three Reformers: Luther, Descartes, Rousseau*, London, Sheed & Ward, 1928.

if we did not find a great deal that is problematic, questionable, worth being questioned; but that is the ambience in which our questioning takes shape, it is in the space of pre-Reformation and pre-Enlightenment Christianity that we find ourselves at home. It is much more important to be able to read Latin and Greek than German or (let's be naughty!) biblical Hebrew!

At this level there are surely two diametrically opposed versions of Western Christianity. What happened at the Reformation, with the expulsion of the legacy of Neoplatonism from Christianity, seems a far deeper problem than most ecumenical discussions recognise. It has to do with radically different understandings of the relationship between reason and faith, nature and grace, Athens and Jerusalem, etc. The test is whether you believe that Christianity started all over again in the sixteenth century, rejecting the Platonism, Aristotelianism, paganism, etc. of what went before, or whether you rejoice that Christianity has absorbed and retained so much from the paganism of the Mediterranean, and above all from Plato. In the latter case, you like the continuities from the pre-Christian to the Christian worlds, and are open to extending them to other non-Christian traditions.

I detect in Radical Orthodoxy writings a desire to overcome, or to sideline, the sixteenth century: to retrieve that biblico-patristic Christian Platonism (exemplified in Augustine and Aquinas) which some of us find it such a pleasure to inhabit – but which, of course, many Reformed Christians find oppressive, superstitious, and pagan.

## VI

Taking that split for granted, then, I have to say that further possibilities of tension and dissent soon arise, as indeed the editors of *Radical Orthodoxy* say at the very beginning of the *Introduction* to the book. Wishing to avoid both "Protestant biblicism" and "post-Tridentine Catholic positivist authoritarianism" as "aberrant results of theological distortions already dominant even before the early modern period" (as suggested above), and never showing any interest in "liberal Protestantism", the editors say that the "perspective" of Radical Orthodoxy is "in profound continuity with the French *nouvelle théologie* which partially undergirded the reforms of Vatican II".

They add, however, that "where radical orthodoxy wishes to reach further is in recovering and extending a fully Christianised ontology and practical philosophy consonant with authentic Christian doctrine".[23]

Steering between Barthian fideism and what Karl Rahner used to call *der Pianische Monolithismus* (Roman Catholic theology from Pius IX to Pius XII), the theologians of *Radical Orthodoxy* want to locate their programme in the wake of the theological movement in French Catholicism which was dubbed the 'new theology' by its bitterest opponents in Rome, and which they hoped was outlawed by Pius XII's encyclical letter *Humani Generis* of 1951.

At this point the story becomes exceedingly complicated. There are, no doubt, Roman Catholics whose 'Catholic response' would be very different from mine. I guess those who admire the tradition of Transcendental Thomism would be unenthusiastic about Radical Orthodoxy. I mean the highly productive and influential version of interpreting Thomas Aquinas in the light of Kant (exemplified by such figures as Pierre Rousselot, Joseph Maréchal, Karl Rahner, J. B. Lotz, and Bernard Lonergan). They built on the assumption that, while Aquinas is the classical theologian of Western Christianity, unavoidably so in the Pian era, his work needs to be, and can fruitfully be, rethought in the light of the Enlightenment and the tradition of German idealism.

It is instructive, however, that, in *Theology and Social Theory*, we find Milbank criticising Rahner on the grounds that, in the interplay of faith and reason, grace and nature, etc., he "naturalises the supernatural". In other words, Rahner pushes his reconstruction of Aquinas "in the direction of a mediating theology, a universal humanism, a *rapprochement* with the Enlightenment and an autonomous secular order".[24] Given that "political theology" in Germany (J. B. Metz) and "liberation theology" in Latin America (Clodovis Boff, Gustavo Gutiérrez) have this tradition in the background, Milbank cannot but reject them – "not without distress", since he realises that his judgement coincides with that of "reactionaries in the Vatican".[25]

Many Catholic theologians, Dominicans in the Cajetanian tradition of Thomism especially, found it hard to accept Henri de Lubac's reinterpretation of Aquinas as a theologian in the line of the patristic tradition that, while

---

23  *Radical Orthodoxy*, p. 2.
24  Milbank, J., *Theology and Social Theory*, p. 207.
25  Milbank, J., *Theology and Social Theory*, p. 208.

stressing natural desire for the vision of God, insists that, in the actual dispensation of salvation, there is no human nature not always already graced.[26] The problem for such theologians (they are best represented these days by the Dominicans at Toulouse and their journal *Revue Thomiste*) was, and still is, that a 'fully Christianised ontology' (etc.) would be an illegitimate obliteration of metaphysics by Scripture, an obliteration of reason and nature by faith and grace.

As Milbank puts it, approvingly, the theologians of the *nouvelle théologie* (he mentions Yves de Montcheuil as well as Henri de Lubac, with Maurice Blondel as the philosopher in the background) in effect "supernaturalise the natural".[27] For their opponents (such as, notably, Réginald Garrigou-Lagrange), this supernaturalising of the natural seemed in danger of collapsing grace and nature into one another: if human beings were by nature always already 'graced', then it would seem as if the created had no intrinsic value of its own and, correspondingly, as if the dispensation of salvation was not as unanticipated and gratuitous as was supposed. Down the line, logically, this seemed to mean that human reasoning, and particularly philosophy and the sciences, could not be self-standing but must necessarily be subordinate to theology. Paradoxically, theologians who might plausibly be charged with 'post-Tridentine Catholic positivist authoritarianism' in questions of doctrine were the very ones most anxious to secure autonomy for philosophy and the sciences, in what of course they conceived of ideally as a harmony between the work of reason and the gift of divine revelation.

This is not the place to start disentangling all these issues; it is just to say that aligning *Radical Orthodoxy* with the *nouvelle théologie* is already to invite more than one Catholic response – to invite, perhaps, incommensurable responses. That *Radical Orthodoxy* wishes to push the *nouvelle théologie* even further in the direction of theology's overcoming of metaphysics cannot but arouse disquiet. Both the inheritors of Transcendental Thomism and the continuators of Cajetanian Thomism, utterly opposed as they still are to one another's viewpoints, would unite to repudiate the project of a 'fully Christianised ontology': whether interested in *rapprochement* with the Enlightenment or determined to return to the thirteenth century, these

26  De Lubac, H., *Surnaturel : Études Historiques*, Paris, Aubier, 1946.
27  Milbank, J., *Theology and Social Theory*, p. 219.

adversaries would not accept the opposition between nihilism and Christian Platonism with which Milbank seems to present us.

Hans Urs von Balthasar often claims that this is the alternative with which we are confronted in the West: Christians would be the only people now who can practice metaphysics; everyone else is bound to be subjectivist, emotivist, relativist, etc. Milbank's sympathy with de Lubac and von Balthasar is plain – though not uncritical: on the contrary, he argues at some length that neither of these two great theologians was able to learn enough from the philosopher Blondel. Though not beyond criticism – he dismissed nihilism too readily as an 'intellectual stance' – Blondel remains the hero of *Theology and Social Theory*: 're-understood as theology' (!), Blondel's philosophy turns out to be 'the boldest exercise in Christian thought of modern times'. The reason for this is that he refuses either to return to Mediæval realism (like the Cajetanian Thomists) or to embrace post-Cartesian idealism (like the Transcendental Thomists). By showing how theology can embrace perspectivism, historicism and pragmatism, Blondel is able to begin to offer an account of "the way things really are" – "a new existential account of the experience of grace".[28]

## VII

More generally, however, among Roman Catholics, across the board, away from Aquinas and Augustine, there is a deep split. It may be characterised roughly like this: is the way to be a Catholic these days to do your best to rethink Catholicism, to recreate Catholic sensibility, devotion, liturgy, and so forth, absorbing positively (and of course discriminatingly) everything that is right and good and true and beautiful in Protestantism, the Enlightenment, and modern thought (from Descartes onwards)? Surely what happened at Vatican II was that at last the Roman Catholic Church accepted the truth of the Reformation? At least that is what I heard from Yves Congar, Louis Bouyer and many others in the 1960's, during and immediately after the Council. Here indeed was a return to the Word of God, to Scripture, to preaching, with a new sense of religious liberty, a concern for human rights, a respect for conscience, and so forth. This included a long forgotten theological pluralism, completely opposed to *der Pianische Monolithismus*, and celebrated recently

28  Milbank, J., *Theology and Social Theory*, p. 217.

in *Fides et Ratio* with (as I was astonished to read) its complimentary allusions to Newman, Rosmini, and Blondel.[29]

Or, to continue this rough sketch, do you say that enough is enough, that we have taken on board more than enough. As T. F. Torrance warned decades ago, our most fashionable theologians only recapitulate Schleiermacher's conclusions. Karl Barth pointed out in *Ad Limina Apostolorum* that with these Catholic attempts to be modern (the slogan, after all, was *"aggiornamento!"* – "get up to date!") we have only bought into liberal Protestantism, with its concomitant individualism. On this reading, modernity is just too dangerous to assimilate, even to negotiate. Look at what has happened to the liturgy, now entirely constructed around rationalist ideals of intelligibility, and, paradoxically, favouring rampant emotionalism. On this version of events, the only solution for the Church is to go post-modern – meaning by that, of course, a return to the pre-modern.

On this latter view, roughly speaking, Catholic theology started catching up with modernity just as modernity was being stripped of its pretensions, and thus displayed all the absurdities of belated trendiness. Somewhere in the 1960's Karl Rahner hoped that Catholic thought would take Descartes and the Enlightenment on board – when many philosophers had already brought out their critiques of modern philosophy: Wittgenstein, Heidegger, Gilbert Ryle, Maurice Merleau Ponty, even Karol Wojtyla with his own brew of Lublin Thomism, Schelerian phenomenology and praxis thinking.

How then do theologians described by this latter sketch embrace the postmodern? Is it through taking the postmodern as a given, along with Nietzsche, Heidegger, Derrida, Don Cupitt, Mark C. Taylor? Or is it rather by a return, *ressourcement*, back to the pre-modern? No doubt the astute reader will recognise the need for a hermeneutics of suspicion as well as of retrieval, but, essentially, this would be a return to Maritain, Gilson, G. K. Chesterton and the *non*-transcendental Thomists, where the task is to seek to retrieve Augustine, pseudo-Denys, biblico-patristic exegesis – and so on. Such a strategy can be followed by a Catholic sympathetically inclined to

---

29  John Paul II, Encyclical Letter *Fides et Ratio*, Vatican, Libreria Editrice Vaticana, 1998, translated as *Faith and Reason*, London, Catholic Truth Society, 1998, §74.

*Radical Orthodoxy*, and even finding a place on the project; but this is a journey that will alienate the pilgrim quite seriously from many – even most – Roman Catholic contemporaries. Indeed, the difference already exists in purely Catholic terms – *Communio* versus *Concilium*. Worlds apart.

# PART III
# RADICAL ORTHODOXY'S
# RETRIEVAL OF
# THEOLOGICAL SITES

Chapter Five

# Radical Orthodoxy
# and the Mediations of Time

Catherine Pickstock

There have been a great many valuable responses to, and criticisms of, the volume of essays produced last year introducing a Radically Orthodox theology. The discussions we here witness and are engaged in are very much welcomed, for they form an integral part of what one might call the 'spirit' of Radical Orthodoxy; for that spirit is precisely a call to look again at things one has too often assumed. Let me offer in this essay, however, a call not to regard Radical Orthodoxy as a discrete edifice which purports to be a stronghold. For it is by no means this. Radical Orthodoxy is a hermeneutic disposition and a style of metaphysical vision; and it is not so much a 'thing' or 'place' as a 'task'. And rather than elucidating the strategies and commonplaces of this 'task', I shall attempt here to engage in its disciplines. But in doing so, I hope also, by default, to answer a particularly recurrent objection to a radically orthodox perspective: if this perspective seeks to look again at the tradition, is it not a nostalgic preoccupation?

I will answer this question quickly now: no; but substantiate it later. But, as an aside, I would like here to add the following points. First, what Radical Orthodoxy seeks to criticise in modernity is not so much its suppression of the past, but rather its suppression of the future, since modernity is primarily characterised by an attempt once and for all to state the eternal structures of finitude. In this way, it erects space above time as a substitute for eternity. Above all, what it seeks is stasis and it fears the past because the passage of the past confronts one with the truth that spatial fixity is a fictional contrivance. Secondly, those traditions of the past are by no means identically recoverable in the present, for they were not homogeneous entities singularly definable and thereby, by dint of some formula or mathesis, replicable in the present day. For the past only existed as part of the forward flow of time, so to cleave lacrimally to it as if it were some lost locus of magnificence is not to be true to the past in its own emergence.

Equally, however, it would be a case of very extreme nostalgia indeed if one were to dismiss these past traditions as part of an irrecoverable forward flow of time, never repeatable, and entirely discontinuous from our world. For to take this view is to place a boundary around an earlier epoch and remove it from the drift of time and diversity; and to do this is again to spatialise time, whereas one of the most central aims of a radically orthodox perspective is to restore time and embodiment to our understanding of reality, and to see history as the manifold and yet analogous epiphany of transcendent truth which abides eternally and yet is seen from our modus in an infinity of refractions. Thus, if there is any kind of epochal boundary separating us from the Middle Ages, then, like all boundaries, it is precisely that which articulates beyond itself, for it must perforce bear the impress of what lies against its outer edge. To put this another way, time is a giving and not a taking away; time's drift gives the past to us, just as it gives us to the past which reaches up through time and mysteriously fulfils itself in our present. To say otherwise is to mistake time for space and to be like the melancholic lover in Kierkegaard's treatise on repetition; for the sad lover can only gaze abjectly towards the lost past, and is doomed forever to disappointment, for his gaze assumes a rupture between the past and present, and sees not the non-identical repetition of the former in the latter.

It follows that a radically orthodox perspective sees time not as something to be lamented or circumvented by means of the instruments of nostalgia, but rather as our very condition of possibility *per se*. For just as the past looked forwards, so also do we; and, like the past, we seek to remember that to look forwards is to be situated in time, which means also to be constituted as much by the past as by the hope of the future. For no co-ordinate of time – past, present, or future – wields supreme sway. For these three are, in equal though asymmetrical measure, eternity's moving image. So, those who offer a criticism of Radical Orthodoxy on the grounds of its alleged nostalgia are misunderstanding our intentions altogether; we are seeking to mediate between finitude and transcendence by way of time. We do not seek to wield some atemporal glimpse of transcendence to shore up something pre-existing in the finite; rather, we seek to insist that our changefulness in time is actually what defines us. Future moments which contingently arrive to us appear to be extra to us, and yet are essential – eventually, they are all we are, even though each single moment is destined to pass away. By embracing this narrative identity in pure reception and seeming loss, we paradoxically have all of a self we can have – or, indeed, more of a self than we can have, since time's gift is entirely by grace; whereas, if we seek more security than this, we have nothing, since time will now operate as pure vengeance without the mercy of its hint in passing of eternity. It is this peculiar relationship to time which I think distances us from both liberals and conservatives, for both these latter tend to invoke theology or the notion of God to underwrite some pre-existing value – whether, for conservatives, some fetish of tradition, or for liberals, some timeless humanist value. Against such positions, we would prefer to emphasise that there are no such pre-established givens, for everything is a never-finished work, which yet discloses what lies invisibly within the interstices of time. Indeed, when we do criticise modernity and identify points in the past when a wrong direction appears to have been taken, what we criticise is precisely the suppression of time and its complexities.

Briefly, indeed, against the related charge that we have lost sight of the practical realm and seek instead to cleave to some arcane, gnomic, and rarefied cabal, one has merely to cite some of our main categories to see a consistent attempt to bring together theory and practice: *poiesis*, motion, liturgy, *dunamis*, repetition, music, friendship, desire, the body, community, difference and so forth. (And as John Milbank has shown, these are not the generalised categories of a liberal perspective, nor the entirely discrete and purely Christian categories of a Neo-orthodox perspective.) I think that this criticism of Radical Orthodoxy as arcane and delphic in its preoccupations issues from a regrettable tendency amongst our critics to trivialise the metaphysical. To allay their fears, however, in what follows I will try to show how a genuinely practicable future means also one which is metaphysical. And I shall proceed not with a call to supplement practice with metaphysics, but more drastically with a demonstration that the most seemingly metaphysically abstruse inquiry demands a completion in concrete practice and immediacy. I begin, moreover, not simply with a metaphysical topic, but with the question of theory as such – in other words, the question of human access to truth. I shall approach this via a discussion of Aquinas' treatment of this topic.[1]

The question of theory seems at first sight an abstract one, because surely our human contingency qualifies our attainment of knowledge? One would suppose that we can never really know anything at all, since the moment we know something, the phenomenon ceases to be that thing almost the very instant of our acquaintance with it. Conversely, is not God's knowledge inscrutably atemporal and remote, disembodied, simple, wholly Mind? Curiously, however, we shall see how this is not the case for the tradition; indeed, we shall see that God's knowledge is itself characterised as the reverse of abstract; in the *Quæstiones Disputatæ: de Veritate* Aquinas compares it to the direct physical knowing of a rustic country bumpkin, and he shows how human knowledge mysteriously participates in that same exalted condition.

First of all, then, the nature of God's knowledge. One might think that because for the tradition God is simple and not subject to change or difference, he must know in a manner wholly other from our manner of knowing things. For surely if human beings are to approximate to God in their knowing of things, they will have to attain to a kind of panoptic glimpse or intellectualisation of all phenomena. If God is pre-eminently Mind, so also we must seek to undo the contribution to our perception of things made by our being embodied and being temporally situated. However, when in his relatively early treatise *de Veritate* Aquinas speaks of knowledge not in epistemological terms – as a static atemporal mirroring of phenomena – but as an ontological event which realises or fulfils the being of things known just as much as it fulfils truth in the knower's mind, one is confronted by a theory of knowledge which seems to accentuate human contingency, changefulness, time-boundness, and otherness from God's manner of knowing.[2] For one here sees that not only are the things known incorporated in time, and perhaps not even worth the knowing, since it seems that they only fully realise their being

1    Some of the arguments which follow were first put forward in the 1999 Aquinas Lecture delivered at Blackfriars in Oxford, and are to be published in *New Blackfriars*. I would like to express my thanks to the Editor of *New Blackfriars*, Fergus Kerr OP, for his kind permission in allowing me to air these arguments again in this chapter.
2    Aquinas, *Quæstiones Disputatæ: de Veritate*, Q. 1, a. 1, resp; Q. 1, a. 4, resp. (All citations are taken from V. J. Bourke's translation, *Disputed Questions on Truth*, Chicago, Chicago University Press, 1952-1954 [3 volumes].)

at the moment of our knowing them, but also the 'real relation' which arises between Being and knowledge accentuates the precipitate freight of all such acts of knowing. For knowing here cannot be relied upon; it is manifestly not at a remove from the fray of time and change. Similarly, Aquinas attends directly to the situatedness of our manner of knowing, when in discussing the transcendentals, he observes that it is because of our modus or finite manner of understanding that we perforce see Being under different aspects.[3] Under one of these aspects (that described by the term Being itself) the things we see seem to us to be discrete and to reside in themselves. For Being's equal proximity to everything, whether genus, species and so forth, indicates a maieutic or private closeness of Being to each thing, and hence of each thing to itself, so that under this aspect all things appear to remain in quietude, distinct from one another and in some sense rather self-absorbed.[4]

But this distinctness of things is not phenomenologically exhaustive. Things, according to our finite modus, also appear to relate to one another. On the one hand, they appear to move outwards from themselves towards other things and towards their ends[5] (hence we find the need of a subtle distinction – from our modus – between Being and the Good); or else, on the other hand, things appear to be in a relationship of formal immanence of other things in oneself that occurs at the moment of knowledge; hence we find the need for the further transcendental determination of Truth.[6] Thus we can see that for Aquinas truth is not at all a matter of detached abstraction, but rather of the specific entry into our minds of certain contingent features and events. It is a matter of the conjoining of ourselves with others in time and space.

One can also mention here another way in which human knowledge seems bound by the qualifications of its finiteness. For weaving in and out of the various modes of our finite perspective are the mediations of a further transcendental, namely Beauty, which seems to bestow itself obliquely upon

3  Aquinas: *de Veritate*, Q. 1, a. 1, resp.; Q. 22, a. 1, ad 12; *Summa Theologiæ* I, 2, Q. 27, a. 1 ad 3; Comm. in I Sent., 31, 2, I, ad 4. Te Velde, R. A., *Participation and Substantiality in Thomas Aquinas*, Leiden, E. J. Brill, 1995, pp. 46-53.
4  Te Velde, R., A., *Participation and Substantiality in Thomas Aquinas*, p. 273.
5  Aquinas, *de Veritate*, Q. 1, a. 1, resp. Te Velde, R. A., *Participation and Substantiality in Thomas Aquinas*, p. 273.
6  Aquinas, *de Veritate*, Q. 1, a. 1, resp. Truth is the *convenientiam unius entis ad aliud*. That *convenientia* is the ontological.

the inter-penetrations of Being, Good, and Truth.[7] First of all, Beauty is mysteriously linked with the self-sufficient integrity of Being, its quietude and self-absorption; secondly, insofar as Beauty is linked with desire (beauty being defined by Thomas as that which pleases or delights), it is crucial to the outgoings or ecstases of the will and the good; and, thirdly, insofar as this is manifest, it is fundamental to Truth.

If the quality of reality perceived through the other transcendentals is always, for our perspective, mediated by the refractions of beauty (that is, qualities of proportion, harmony, clarity, integrity), then it seems that everything we claim to know is by definition crossed-out by the fact that, although these beautiful proportions pertain, we cannot ever assess them as it were from a neutral measurable distance.[8] For beauty is something immanently disclosed through something else in an unmeasurable way, and so points us to an unavoidable problem of all human knowledge: there is nothing of which one can be certain; if knowledge has always an aesthetic moment, then anything that is known is not known at all, but only judged on the basis of beauty. If knowledge is no more than a matter of judgement, then all human strivings for truth are doomed from the outset.

For a number of reasons, therefore, it seems that Aquinas brutally qualifies the possible attainments of human knowledge; it is time-bound, subjective, diverse, limited, and fraught with bias. And yet, must we assume no continuity at all between the way we know things and the way they are? Is human knowledge entirely fantastical? It seems that things are not necessarily so bad, for at this point Aquinas introduces a further refraction of Being, namely the Soul, which links everything together, not in the manner of an after-thought, as it were, once the private closeness of Being to distinct things has been established, for these aspects of Being do not unfold successively, but rather, primordially.[9] It is rather the case that these distinct things simply would not be fully realised in their formal potential without the Soul's knowing of them; thus Being is by no means prior to knowing, nor knowing prior to Being; the one measures the other in such a way as to suggest a kind of ideal realism which furnishes us with a manner of continuity between the

---

7   See further, Milbank, J., and Pickstock, C., *Truth in Aquinas*, London, Routledge (forthcoming), chapter 1.
8   Aquinas, *Summa Theologiæ*, I, 1, Q. 5, a. 1.
9   Aquinas, *de Veritate*, Q. 1, a. 1, resp.

way things are in the external material world and the way things are in our mind.

And yet we must not construe this continuity in the manner, say, of a modern correspondence theory. It is not for Aquinas a continuity in the sense of a mirroring, of our thoughts simply being 'true to the facts'. Rather, this continuity is a 'real relation' whereby our thought occasions a teleological realisation of the formality of things, and, in doing so, is itself brought to fruition. Thus, building upon Augustine's *topos* that thought is 'a higher kind of life', we see that intellection is not an indifferent speculation, but a beautiful ratio instantiated between things and the mind which leaves neither thing nor mind unchanged. We see also that it has become virtually impossible to say whether Aquinas' theory of human knowledge is ruefully pessimistic or rather ecstatically optimistic, because it now seems that, despite all the problems mentioned in the foregoing, knowing-a-thing, insofar as it occasions the teleological fruition of the thing known, is an act of generosity or salvific compensation for the discreteness of things.[10] But here one should point out that this realisation in the human mind of a thing known is but an intermediate stage to the optimum realisation of things in the Mind of God. And so a thing is fulfilling its *telos* when it is copying God in its own appointed manner, and tending to existence in the divine Mind: so a willow copies God by being true to its willowness, rain by being rainy, and a stone by being stony, to give Aquinas' own example.

But if all things are subordinated to the divine intellect in this way, does this after all mean that we fall back upon a humiliation of all human strivings for knowledge, that here we have a theory of truth which has no essential recourse to an encounter with the way things actually are? Certainly, there is an idealist aspect here; and yet, the very referral to the divine intellect reveals a concept of understanding not as an unfolding of a priori truths, but as an orientation towards the ideal as embodied in actuality. And it is here that we begin to see that Aquinas' referral of human knowledge to transcendence is one and the same with a referral to embodiment, actuality and time.

How can this be? There are several reasons. The first is this, that as Aquinas observes, since God's self-knowledge is perforce simple, it must

---

10  Aquinas, *de Veritate*, Q. 2, a. 2; Q. 4, a. 2, resp.; Q. 10, a. 1, resp.; Blanchette, O., *The Perfection of the Universe According to Aquinas: A Teleological Cosmology*, Pennsylvania, Pennsylvania State University Press, 1992, pp. 270-279, pp. 291-296.

exceed the distinction between formal and material. It is not, as for Aristotle, the abstract metaphysical knowledge of the first mover, but rather the knowledge of a craftsman or artisan, for whom 'idea' extends to the entire conception of the realised product.[11] Thus God's idea is realised in the work of his emanating *verbum*, which although eternal and unchanging – is nonetheless a real production. One can note here that only with the doctrine of creation does one really arrive at the idea that God knows material particulars. In Aristotle, things become known only to the degree that they are abstracted from matter. This of course remains true for Aquinas, and yet Aquinas gives this *topos* an entirely different turn, by declaring that God has an idea of matter and of material things as limited participations in His own Mind. It is thus the Platonic notion of participation which perhaps surprisingly allows a more elevated notion of matter. Even before elaborating a Trinitarian theology, Aquinas introduces a note of relationality and difference, for he speaks of God's knowledge of all the modes in which He can be participated in their exact material details. In the manner of an artisan, then, God knows His creation fully in knowing the ends of its component parts, their manifold perfections, which include all that they actually are.

We have seen, so far, that human knowledge, though coloured by situatedness, time and judgement, and subordinated to the divine Mind, is nonetheless able to draw analogically towards God's manner of knowing, for the latter, in surpassing the distinction of formal and material knowing, is not inimical to a craft-like and relational expressiveness, nor is it oblivious to the unique material differentiations of creation. In fact, one could mention here a further perhaps more shocking way in which human knowledge draws near to God's manner of knowing. I have indicated already that, following Aristotle, the Soul, insofar as it is in a manner all things, is a primordial refraction of Being, and so is fundamental in mediating between knowledge and Being. This, we have seen, means that our knowledge hovers between idealist and realist criteria, and we have also seen (in an analogical fashion) that this is not so very unlike God's manner of knowing. Crucially, Aquinas regards intellect as a power of the soul, rather than its essence.[12] What this

---

11　Aquinas, *de Veritate*, Q. 1, a. 2; Aquinas, *Summa Theologiæ*, I, 1: Q. 1, a. 2, a. 3, a. 5; Q. 14, a. 16; Q. 15, a. 2, ad 2; Q. 16, a. 6.

12　Aquinas, *DeVeritate*, Q. 2, a. 1; Q. 12, a. 1, a. 2; Q. 12, a. 13, resp.; Aquinas, *Summa Theologiæ*, I, 1, Q. 79, a. 1, resp.

means is that in a most daring fashion Aquinas sees the power of the mind as in some way accidental to us, in the manner of an oxymoronic 'proper accident': 'proper' because intellect defines what we are; yet 'accidental', because it arises super-essentially; and 'oxymoronic', because what I have just said seems entirely devoid of sense – namely, that intellect is essential to us and yet super-essential to us. It is as if to say that the human animal need not 'think', but only when it does, is it really human, and the more it exercises intellect, the more human it becomes.

To say that intellection is, as it were, a borrowed power might seem to downgrade the mind. But, if anything, the reverse is the case. For Aquinas here deploys the Neoplatonic metaphysics of participation to show that he regards our capacity for thought not as a ruefully humiliated endeavour, but as a partial receiving of divine intellection on a transcendental level. Thus, it seems that what is extra to us, namely, intellection, most defines us in the act of knowing. This contradiction points us in fact to the workings of grace, which is what enables us to exceed ourselves. And here one can assert a further contradiction, for it seems that it is precisely the difference between God's manner of knowing and our own, which makes our manner of knowing, in a strange and entirely humble way, God-like. For God, as cause of knowing, is in Himself super-abundantly knowing, and is not simply a wholly inscrutable and unknown cause of our knowledge. For this reason, we can know something – albeit remotely – of God's knowing of Himself. That is to say, we can analogically predicate knowledge of God. Although our own imitations of God's knowledge are always marked by imperfection and diversity, even here what seems a deficiency in our modus in fact betokens its own remedy.

We have seen, then, several ways in which our knowledge draws near to God's manner of knowing, and that those very things which might seem to distance our knowledge from that of God – such as its temporal nature, diversity and material relationships – in fact draw us nearer still. But there remains one seemingly insurmountable difference, which is that although God is pure Mind without remainder, and therefore a more spiritual kind of knower than human beings, nevertheless, His knowledge is more concrete than ours.[13] This is because when we know a thing, we cannot directly apprehend its

---

13  Aquinas, *de Veritate*, Q. 2, a. 1, resp.; Q. 2, a. 5 resp.; Aquinas, *Summa Theologiæ*, I, 1, Q. 16, a. 1, resp.

material individuation, for, following Aristotle, matter cannot enter the human intellect. The limits of one's intellect keep pace with one's capacity to produce. Just as we can produce a form in things like a craftsman, so also we can know forms. But we cannot produce matter with our intellect, and so we cannot know matter. By contrast, Aquinas actually says that God is much more of a country bumpkin capable of a brutal direct unreflective intuition of cloddish earth, bleared and smeared with toil.[14] For God's mind, although immaterial, is mysteriously commensurate with matter, since God creates matter. And because he makes matter, so also he knows it.

It seems then that despite the graceful accident of our capacity to know beyond our natures, we cannot aspire to the noble estate of bumpkinhood where material singulars can be espied in all their brutishness – that after all, for the tradition, human knowledge is a rarefied and abstract thing. Or is it? It seems that a token bumpkinhood is not denied us. Beyond Aristotle, Aquinas develops an account of how we do in a certain measure participate in the divine knowledge of singulars. Whilst God knows material things precisely because he is timelessly outside them and brings them to be from nothing, Aquinas stresses that it is our very timeliness which draws us close to God's manner of knowing concrete things. In fact, it is because human knowledge is a kind of movement or motion – something which one would think betokened our complete lack of Godlikeness – which accomplishes this proximity.

Briefly, then, what is the movement of human knowledge? When we seek to know a concrete singular thing, let us say a cricket bat, the form of the bat leaves its substance and becomes an abstract species. It travels through the human senses, then through the imagination, and finally into the mind of the observer. So far, Aquinas is drawing upon Aristotle's theory of knowledge, which does not get us very near a concrete or God-like way of knowing. But when the species enters the passive intellect, it is articulated or expressed by the active intellect, and the product of this expression, Aquinas (following Augustine) describes as *verbum*, or inner word.[15] This *verbum* or inner word acts in the manner of a sign, pointing away from itself, back to what it represents – that is, if we recall, a cricket bat. Thus, intellect as intention fuses with desire since to intend something is also to desire to know more of the

14  Aquinas, *de Veritate*, Q. 2, a. 5, resp.
15  Aquinas, *de Veritate*, Q. 4, a. 1, resp.

truth of that thing – this goal being regarded as a good. However, despite this operation of desire which points us back to what the *verbum* is expressing, we still cannot say we know the cricket bat in any God– or bumpkin-like way, for however much the sign or *verbum* might seem to mediate the concrete, the latter still cannot enter our mind. At this point, Aquinas develops a theory of the imagination – long before Kant – and it is here that a fusion of sense and intellect begins to occur. Interestingly, imagination is somehow something one is not aware of when it is operating; it is something one peers through, without consciousness of a mediating principle. This oblique mediating principle provides a mysterious echo of material sensing within the intellect, and in this fashion we attain inchoately to a bumpkin-like state of knowing, for we 'feel' or 'imagine' a concrete knowledge of the cricket bat, and, by virtue of the transparency of mediation, its presence in our intellect is mysteriously more than simply a fiction or figment. Because for Aquinas truth 'corresponds' not by copying but by a new analogical realisation of something in the mind in an inscrutable 'proportion' to how it is in reality, the imagination can act creatively without fictional betrayal; indeed, must act creatively if it is to be 'true'.

Thus, just as we have seen that the act of intellection is accidental and yet proper to us, so now we see that in the exercise of our imagination, which is the ecstatic principle by which we overcome the limits of our capacity to produce and hence know material singulars, those features which most differentiate us from God – diversity, time, feelings, modes, contingencies, mediations – furnish us with the means by which analogically to penetrate that difference. We see also that where it might seem that Aquinas stresses the difference and distance of human knowing, it seems that we know by participation in divine knowledge, and moreover that this relation to the above is mediated by our turning to the world below and cleaving to our limitations.

We have seen, then, that to attain to the highest things, we must not retreat from the world, but engage with it and receive it fully. However, if our knowledge has a practical aspect, and if the mundane domain can furnish us with the means to draw near to God, that is precisely because this domain is only suspended from the divine height. If there can be correspondence of thought to beings, this is only because, more fundamentally, both beings and minds correspond to the divine *esse* and *mens* or intellect. Thus correspondence for Aquinas is of what we know according to our finite modus to God who is intrinsically far more knowable, and yet to us in His essence, utterly unknown.    This means that rather than correspondence being guaranteed in its measuring of the given, as for modern notions of correspondence, rather it is guaranteed by its conformation to the divine source of the given.   While to advance to this source is of course to advance in unknowing, it is only in terms of this unknowing, increased through faith, that we confirm even our ordinary knowing of finite things.

Moreover this confirmation by conformation to the unknown divine mind is far more emphatic in its claim than simply an analogical drawing-near or resemblance.   It is an assimilation, an ontological impress which moulds or contrives the very forms of things.   But what is 'contrived' or brought to pass occurs transparently; like the invisible mediations of beauty, we look through this 'making' without seeing it, even as we know beyond ourselves by means of it; we forget that what we know is more than we can possibly know.   And, moreover, even when we are knowing ordinary temporal things, straining to be like bumpkins apprehending a lunar eclipse, even then, at such a moment of lowly endeavour, the motions of our intellect and of our will vastly exceed their capacity, and mould themselves into the idiom of the procession of the eternal Word from the Father, and that of the Holy Spirit from the Father and the Son.   Thus, just as for Aquinas, to correspond in knowing is to be conformed to the infinite unknown, so likewise our knowing of anything at all is in some measure an advance sight of the beatific vision, and union with the personal interplay of the Trinity.[16]

Finally, I would like to position the foregoing in relation to my opening remarks about the centrality for Radical Orthodoxy of, first, the mediations of time and the body, and, secondly, of metaphysical considerations.   We have seen a recurrent pattern whereby the spiritually remote and the materially ultimate paradoxically reinforce each other.   And it is the inescapability of this pattern which justifies and indeed requires the most rigorous and seemingly abstruse theological inquiry.   For only the most rigorous thought is able to think the insufficiency of pure thought alone and thus to head off a gnosticism which thinks one can attain wisdom purely at an intellectual level.   Such a position must be defeated if one is to see that one can only attain to a foretaste of the beatific vision through the sensory and the material.   Equally, it must

---

16  Aquinas, *de Veritate*, Q. 4, a. 4, resp. For a fuller discussion of the above mentioned arguments, see Milbank, J., and Pickstock, C., *Truth in Aquinas*.

be defeated if one is not going to separate off ordinary life from worship of the divine, leaving it abandoned to the closed triviality of the secular, in neglect of its own intrinsic potential for the highest insight.

# Chapter Six

# Quod Impossibile Est!
# Aquinas and Radical Orthodoxy

Laurence Paul Hemming

It may seem a little odd, compared to the other discussions in this book, that this middle dialogue is between Catherine Pickstock and myself, who were both contributors to the *Radical Orthodoxy* volume. Yet mine has been, although tolerated, an uneasy voice in the *Radical Orthodoxy* project, for reasons that I want to make explicit. I pose these reasons as a challenge, generously intended, to the editors of *Radical Orthodoxy* (and as they have each now styled it, Radical Orthodoxy, by which they clearly intend something wider and more far-reaching than the book alone). *Radical Orthodoxy* authors have assumed a certain Catholic voice, above all in their unquestioning appropriation of St. Thomas Aquinas. Whereas so eminent a Thomist as the Anglican E. L. Mascall felt the need carefully to locate his interest within the broader context of Aquinas' exponents, the impression has been given (and strongly intended) that *Radical Orthodoxy* need have no such qualms.[1]

It is this appropriation of Aquinas that has led to the accusation that Radical Orthodoxy indulges in a nostalgia towards Mediæval authors. The suggestion is that this inventive appropriation of Mediæval authors seems somewhat dislocated, or even ahistorical. John Milbank and Catherine Pickstock have in their turn often given the impression (and I believe that I am only slightly caricaturing it here) that if 'modernity' or the rationalism of the Enlightenment were bracketed out, a certain return to something prior to it

---

1 Cf. for instance, Mascall, E. L., *The Openness of Being*, London, DLT, 1971, pp. 11-14 (the Gifford Lectures, 1970-71). Mascall takes some care to locate himself within the context of the "neo-thomists", amongst whom he counts Gilson, and the Transcendental Thomists: Rahner; Coreth; and Lotz; and the man whom he refers to as the "philosopher's philosopher" and "theologian's theologian" (and who is "untainted" by the influence of Heidegger), Bernard Lonergan.

could be opened up. That 'something prior' is best exemplified for Radical Orthodoxy by Aquinas. Moreover their claim has strongly been supported by a widespread return to the study of Aquinas by a substantial number of English-speaking, mainly Catholic, authors.[2] My argument in this chapter, however, is that it is just in their articulation of Aquinas that what is most cavalier and hazardous about Radical Orthodoxy can be seen most clearly at work.

Gareth Jones' review of *Radical Orthodoxy* illustrates well my concerns. He acclaims the "genuine intellectual achievement" of John Milbank's work, which *Radical Orthodoxy* at its best also shares, but goes on to mention his "substantial difficulties with the entire project". The sharpest criticism of the three he advances is that "this book is distinguished by an entirely ahistorical engagement with ideas and their production".[3] Catherine Pickstock's contribution to this collection of essays is a case in point. She elaborates an engaging and compelling reading of Aquinas. Her contribution, *Radical Orthodoxy and the Mediations of Time*, takes as its central example a comparison between our knowledge, and God's knowledge. To compare, as

2   The work of David Burrell, a contributor to this volume, would be a case in point. (Burrell, D., *Knowing the Unknowable God: Ibn-Sina, Maimonides, Aquinas*, Indiana, University of Notre Dame Press, 1986; and *Aquinas: God and Action*, London, Routledge and Kegan Paul, 1979; to name only two.)   Just two more of the many North Americans who participate in this revival are Mark Jordan (Jordan, M. D.: *The Alleged Aristotelianism of Thomas Aquinas*, Toronto, Pontifical Institute of Mediæval Studies, 1992; *Ordering Wisdom: the Hierarchy of Philosophical Discourses in Aquinas*, Indiana, University of Notre Dame Press, 1986, again being only two examples of his extensive work) as well as non-Catholics like A. N. Williams (cf. for example *Mystical Theology Redux: The Pattern of Aquinas' Summa Theologiæ* in *Modern Theology*, April 1997, Vol. 13, No. 1). In the United Kingdom interest in Aquinas has tended to come mainly through thinkers influenced by analytic philosophy (like Richard Swinburne and, in a different style, Brian Davies OP), but see also Moonan, L., *Divine Power: the Medieval Power Distinction up to its Adoption by Albert, Bonaventure, and Aquinas*, Oxford, Oxford University Press, 1994; in Ireland the important work of Fran O'Rourke has resulted in texts like O'Rourke, F., *Pseudo-Dionysius & the Metaphysics of Aquinas*, Leiden, E. J. Brill, 1992, and *The Gift of Being: Heidegger and Aquinas* in O'Rourke, F. (ed.), *At the Heart of the Real*, Dublin, Irish Academic Press, 1992.

3   Cf. Jones, G., *On Not Seeing the Joke*, review of *Radical Orthodoxy* in *Times Literary Supplement [TLS]*, April 2nd, 1999, p. 12.

she does, God's knowledge to that of a "country bumpkin" or "*rusticus*"[4] *over against* our own more trammelled wisdom is an elegant and creative conceit. The knowledge of scholars is compared with the simple knowledge that is both God's and a country bumpkin's: in this way the dangers inherent in our very sophistication are thrown into relief.

Cleverly put, nevertheless this is a central plank of Radical Orthodoxy's programme: all the dogged work of thinking myself into the work of Aquinas, which requires painstaking study, a knowledge of sources and a comportment of humility before his greater understanding, taken together with the difficult realisation that I may just make mistakes and draw wrong conclusions – all this is not necessary. If, rather, I just see with an unstudied immediacy what Aquinas himself saw, then I join with Aquinas in knowing what God intended for both of us to know. The exalted flash of insight is always preferred: moreover, in looking at what Aquinas looked at, and so seeing what he saw, I do not have to take into account who I am in regard to Aquinas. The distance between us is collapsed in the same way as the distance between myself and God.

The problem is that this view, which is claimed as entirely representative of Aquinas, is indeed no more than a conceit. As I shall show, it entirely misrepresents Aquinas' own concerns. If we overlook the ambiguous notion of simplicity at work here (lest we make of God a simpleton), the question at issue, for Pickstock and for Aquinas, is God's knowledge of singulars – particular things or events: this book, that eclipse of the moon. In Question Two of Aquinas' *Questiones Disputatæ: de Veritate* where he asks *Whether God knows Singulars*,[5] Aquinas is in dialogue with Avicenna, and the dialogue concerns Book XII of Aristotle's *Metaphysics*, which itself takes up the question of how an understanding, or view, of substance can be gained.[6] The Greek verb at issue is θεωρεῖν, to take a view, or to behold in contemplation. What is at issue, therefore, is discernment itself. Aquinas presents Avicenna's understanding of whether God has knowledge of singulars in the following

---

4    See Pickstock, C., *Radical Orthodoxy and the Mediations of Time* (above), p. 66. The term "country bumpkin" translates Aquinas' term "rusticus", and is taken from V. J. Bourke's translation of Aquinas *Quæstiones Disputatæ: de Veritate*, published as *Disputed Questions on Truth*, Chicago, Chicago University Press, 1952-4, Vol. I, p. 87 f.

5    Aquinas, *Quæstiones Disputatæ: de Veritate*, Q. 2, a. 5, *Utrum Deus Cognoscat Singularia*.

6    Aristotle, *Metaphysics*, XII, 1069a. "Περὶ τῆς οὐσίας ἡ θεωρία."

way: God knows every singular through its universal.[7] The example Aquinas uses reflects Aristotle's own reference to viewing and beholding in 'seeing' through the verb θεωρεῖν. Aquinas uses the example of how an astronomer, knowing all the motions of the heavens through observing their movements, would know every eclipse that is to occur for the next hundred years. This knowing, which is theoretical, is entirely different to the kind of knowing which *rusticus*, the country bumpkin, would have if he were simply to see an eclipse, for this latter knowledge is not theoretical (and so predictive), but immediate, though also *seen*. The point at issue concerns how *rusticus* sees: the text says "sicut rusticus cognoscit dum eam videt": "as a bumpkin knows when he *sees*".[8] The contrast between *rusticus* and the astronomer is drawn to distinguish between knowledge of singulars and universals which is gained by, and extrapolated from, *looking* at things. Looking here already contains distance from what is looked *at*.

What Pickstock overlooks, in claiming that Aquinas opts for the way the bumpkin knows as the one closest to God, is that Aquinas argues that God knows in the manner of both *rusticus* and the astronomer. He says that "God knows all singulars, not only in their universal causes but *also* each in its proper and singular nature".[9] This is preparatory to his dismissal of *both* 'views' as inadequate properly to describe God's knowledge; the better and more informative example, he says, is to understand God's knowledge by comparing it to the knowledge a craftsperson or artificer has of what he or she crafts.[10] This order of example which Aquinas is so careful to set up is, however, exactly reversed by Pickstock, when she says:

> Just as we can produce a form in things, like a craftsman, so also we can know forms. But we cannot produce matter with our intellect, and so we cannot know matter. By contrast, Aquinas actually says that God is much

7  Aquinas, *de Veritate*, Q. 2, a. 5, resp. "Dix[it] Avicenna ... quod Deus unumquodque singularium cognoscit quasi in universali."
8  My emphasis.
9  Aquinas, *de Veritate*, Q. 2, a. 5, resp. "... quod Deus singularia cognoscat non solum in universalibus causis, sed etiam unumquodque secundum propriam et singularem naturam."
10 Aquinas, *de Veritate*, Q. 2, a. 5, resp. (following immediately from the sentence in note seven above). "Ad cuius evidentiam sciendum, quod scientia divina, quam de rebus habet, comparatur scientiæ artificis, eo quod est causa omnium rerum, sicut ars artificiatorum."

more of a country bumpkin capable of a brutal direct unreflective intuition of cloddish earth, bleared and smeared with toil.[11]

Pickstock characterises the bumpkin as one "smeared with toil", although Aquinas makes no reference to toil, being solely concerned with what *rusticus* sees. This is because *rusticus* is at the very best the experienced worker in toil, the ἔμπειρος referred to by Aristotle; one who creates because he or she has a certain experience in toil, and who brings the artificer's vision to fruition in a thing, or creation.[12] He or she sees by looking *at*.

Book XII of Aristotle's *Metaphysics* is, as I have argued, concerned with the relation of contemplation (θεωρεῖν) to substance (οὐσία). However, it is the origins and causes of substance that are at issue.[13] The ἔμπειρος is more distant from causes and origins; he or she is the one who simply brings the thing to fruition through familiarity and closeness to the material nature of it, without understanding or having any theories about it: he or she relates to things only as singulars. It is this closeness to the material nature (through familiarity) that Pickstock exploits in her use of the example. However, the artificer, or τεχνήτης, is the one charged with knowing and understanding the higher causes of an exterior production, because he or she is causing it to be at all: creating not through toil, but through an originating causation, which therefore relates *both* to singulars (insofar as he or she is charged with creating a particular thing) *and* to universals (insofar as the artificer understands how to create any thing at all).[14]

Whereas *rusticus* looks *at* in order to be close and familiar, the artificer creates the picture which will become what is looked at. The artificer can look

---

11  Pickstock, C., *Radical Orthodoxy and the Mediations of Time*, p. 72.

12  For this distinction in Aristotle, see *Metaphysics*, I, 981a25. "καὶ σοφωτέους τοὺς τεχνίτας τῶν ἐμπείρων ὑπολαμβάνομεν ..." ["We assume artificers are wiser than experienced people."] Aquinas was well aware of the distinction Aristotle makes here: he comments on it in *In Libros Metaphysicorum*, I, lect. 1, n. 18.

13  Aristotle, *Metaphysics*, XII, 1069a18. "τῶν γὰρ οὐσιῶν αἱ ἀρχαὶ καὶ τὰ αἴτια ζητοῦνται."

14  Cf. Aquinas, *In Libros Metaphysicorum*, I, lect. 1, n. 17. Experience (ἔμπειρια) and art (τεχνή) "differ inasmuch as universals are grasped by art and singular things by experience". [" ... dissimilitudo autem, quia per artem accipiuntur universalia, per experimentum singularia, ut postea dicetur".]

*at*, but more importantly (and more wisely) originates by causing what is *to be looked at* in the first place. This is the closeness, not of familiarity, but of having caused to be at all.

For Aristotle, and for Aquinas following him and commenting on him, neither the highest contemplation of the heavens (θεωρεῖν) for the sake of the universals by an astronomer, nor the direct familiar and close seeing of a singular by a rustic bumpkin (ἔμπειρος) really indicate for Aquinas the nature of God's knowledge. Both contemplation and immediate seeing are different means of discerning causes by looking *at* something. Neither compare with the knowing that is given through being the originating (ἀρχή) cause *of* something, where what was intended in the cause is already known and so does not need to be discerned. Here knowing by intending is prior to looking to discover what was intended. This is the real reason for Aquinas surpassing the knowledge of the astronomer or the bumpkin with that of the artificer in his example.

Pickstock tells us "beyond Aristotle, Aquinas develops an account of how we do in a certain measure participate in the divine knowledge of singulars".[15] My argument is the reverse: I have shown that Aquinas' argument is not moving beyond, but *entirely* within the province of Aristotle's own understanding of truth. This has additional consequences we shall explore later.

Most particularly, in debate with Avicenna (which I have already indicated is the backdrop to the example from which Pickstock draws the example of the bumpkin), Aquinas would have to be sure of his ground with respect to Aristotle. If it is through Aristotle that Aquinas conducted his debate with the Arab scholars, this is because he received much of Aristotle from Arab hands. Aquinas' use of Aristotle therefore has an apologetic aspect. He could not possibly have privileged the knowing of a *rusticus* over the knowing of one who produces through craft because to do so would have been to depart from (and in fact reverse) the structure of knowledge and wisdom that Aristotle describes in the *Metaphysics* and the *Nichomachean Ethics*, to which Aquinas must adhere to in order to demonstrate the intellectual coherence and superiority of Christian faith in the face of powerful Arab scholarship.

If what Aquinas intended in his example of the *rusticus* is now perhaps clearer, and it is also clear that Pickstock has profoundly altered that intention,

15 Pickstock, C., *Radical Orthodoxy and the Mediations of Time*, p. 72.

what are we to make of her claim that the Aquinas she presents is the Aquinas of Radical Orthodoxy? What does Pickstock herself intend through citing Aquinas? I do not believe that the solution lies simply in any accusation of poverty of scholarship, but rather that something else is at work. She says "we cannot aspire to the noble estate of bumpkinhood", however, "it seems that a token bumpkinhood is not denied us".[16]

The key to understanding Pickstock's analysis is in the phrase "noble estate of bumpkinhood", for she is making claims about immediacy of knowledge through an appeal to rusticity as the guarantor of her argument. Aquinas makes no such claims about the rustic bumpkin. Indeed, for him, bumpkins and astronomers are alike in relation to God and God's knowledge: they are equally remote from God's greater immediacy to the things God has created. Aquinas has no elevated view of bumpkins. If my reading of Aquinas is correct, both he and the humble *rusticus* are being put into service for the sake of something else. Radical Orthodoxy constantly seeks through these kinds of moves to install a linguistic immediacy where terms simply mean what they are declared to mean. Any diversity of meaning in a term is subordinated to its 'true' or 'immediate' meaning. Language thereby installs truth by assertion. Truth is acquired through single, simple, intellective acts, which are then declared to be co-extensive with the mind of God.

Aquinas is simply being co-opted as an authority for this view. The noble bumpkin here is none other than the no less noble savage of French Rationalism, and this practice is none other than G. E. Moore's naturalistic fallacy. Indeed, Moore warns us that "the naturalistic fallacy has been quite as commonly committed with regard to beauty as with regard to good: its use has introduced as many errors into Aesthetics as into Ethics".[17] The appeal to the bumpkin, from whom we scholars are clearly estranged, is therefore used to displace what we would otherwise take to be true: that terms are complex and must be thought *about* to be understood. In short, human knowledge of

---

16  Pickstock, C., *Radical Orthodoxy and the Mediations of Time*, p. 72.
17  More, G. E., *Principia Ethica*, Cambridge, Cambridge University Press, 1903, p. 201. Exactly the same criticism can be made of John Milbank's appeal to "romantic love" in the Chapter Three above, p. 45. It is simply bizarre to re-inaugurate a notion of romantic love without any reference to, or perspicacity towards, the extensive investigations of feminist writers and work in the area of gender identity, as if a simple reference to power and domination will suffice to cover all. This does not mean one is forced to agree with all or any of what has been written, rather that what has been said cannot so lightly be dismissed.

God or of the natural world cannot escape the exercise of discernment, or what Aristotle called θεωρεῖν. Radical Orthodoxy in general, and Pickstock in particular, are arguing that what for them is the simplest and most immediate meaning of a term (what they *declare* it to be) is indeed its truth.

Radical Orthodoxy could, however, defend the appeal to Aquinas by reference to an unimpeachably Catholic tradition. In 1879 Pope Leo XIII called for the restoration of the pre-eminence of the works of Aquinas, in the Apostolic Letter *Æterni Patris*, a restoration that spawned not one, but repeated re-engagements with the Angelic Doctor – from the worthy tomes of Thomism now gathering dust in seminaries to Transcendental Thomism, from Chenu to 'Existential Thomism' and beyond. This engagement has been encouraged by successive Papal pronouncements, and in repeated references to Aquinas in Vatican documents. Pope Paul VI renewed the wishes of Leo XIII in the letter *Lumen Ecclesiæ*, and most recently Pope John Paul II's encyclical *Fides et Ratio* confirmed the continuing importance of Aquinas.

The difficulty, however, is that from *Æterni Patris* to the present the demand of the Magisterium has been for a restoration of not *theology* but *philosophy*. Radical Orthodoxy, in contrast, has wanted to speak emphatically of Thomas' *theological* voice, and more generally of theology evacuating philosophy,[18] – indeed Catherine herself tells us at the very outset of *After Writing* that her work "completes and surpasses philosophy".[19] Leo XIII, in contrast, envisaged the mutuality of the two, going so far as to say "the Church herself not only urges, but even commands, Christian teachers to seek help from philosophy".[20] John Paul II, citing the *Summa Theologiæ* says, "all

---

18  Cf. John Milbank's claim that "where Scotus inaugurated a metaphysics independent of theology, Eckhart absolutely evacuated the metaphysical site in favour of theology". Milbank, J., *Only Theology overcomes Metaphysics*, New Blackfriars, July/August 1995, p. 335. (Reprinted in *The Word Made Strange*, Oxford, Blackwell, 1997, p. 45.) Cf. also p. 49, where Milbank again speaks of "evacuation", adding "An independent phenomenology must be given up, along with the claim, which would have seemed so bizarre to the fathers, to be doing philosophy *as well as* theology". (Author's emphasis.)

19  Pickstock, C., *After Writing: The Liturgical Consummation of Philosophy*, Oxford, Blackwell, 1997, p. xii.

20  Leo XIII, Apostolic Letter *Æterni Patris*, Vatican, Libreria Editrice Vaticana, 1879, §7. "The Church herself not only urges, but even commands, Christian teachers to seek help from philosophy."

truth, however spoken, is of the Holy Spirit",[21] and speaks of the complementarity of theological and philosophical wisdom.

It has been precisely because they perceived a certain crisis of reason that the Popes have called for philosophy's restoration. In a separate Encyclical, *Quod Apostolici Muneris* in 1878, Leo XIII traced the whole history of Ecclesial protest against the demise of reason.[22] John Paul II's more recent diagnosis of that crisis uses language often quite close (but in fact not co-extensive on these very points) to Radical Orthodoxy's.[23] He speaks of how "as a result of the crisis of rationalism, what has appeared finally is *nihilism*".[24] He traces this as the effect of an instrumentalisation of philosophy – in other words of philosophy's abandoning of its proper task for the sake of something else, and how philosophy has been perverted towards the promotion of utilitarian ends, or the ends of enjoyment or domination.[25]

My problem with Radical Orthodoxy's use of Aquinas is that it exactly corresponds to the instrumentalisation of reason against which *Fides et Ratio* protests. Aquinas is put into service for the sake of something else, namely that rather than undertake the difficult genealogical enquiry into the crisis of reason which is required in order both to understand it and to answer it with the generous perspicacity it deserves, reason can simply be declared once again to be 'true', if only in 'theology'.

In consequence, whilst the Radical Orthodoxy position is vocally cognisant of the crisis of which John Paul II speaks, its exponents have missed the point, and taken what philosophy itself delineates and describes for what philosophy

---

21  John Paul II, Encyclical Letter *Fides et Ratio*, Vatican, Libreria Editrice Vaticana, 1998, §44, quoting Aquinas, *Summa Theologiæ*, I, 1, 2, Q. 109, Art. 1 ad. 1. "Omne verum a quocumque dicatur a Spiritu Sancto est."

22  Leo XIII, Encyclical Letter *Quod Apostolici Muneris*, Vatican, Libreria Editrice Vaticana, 1878.

23  See the critique elaborated in *Radical Orthodoxy*, pp. 2-4. The crisis of reason is summed up here as follows: "The fact of [the tradition's] late Mediæval collapse ... the Enlightenment was in effect a critique of decadent early modern Christianity, it *is* sometimes possible to learn from it, though in the end the Enlightenment itself massively repeated the decadence" (p. 2 f.). (Author's emphasis).

24  John Paul II, *Fides et Ratio*, §46. "Veluti consequens discriminis rationalismi tandem *nihilismus* crevit." (Author's emphasis.)

25  John Paul II, *Fides et Ratio*, §47. "Pro veritatis contemplatione atque finis ultimi sensusque vitae inquisitione, formae hae rationalitatis diriguntur – vel saltem sunt convertibiles – veluti 'rationes instrumentales', quae inserviant utilitatis propositis, voluptatibus vel dominationi."

actually *is*. In consequence they have called for the surpassing and evacuation of philosophy *against* its restoration. Now if all that was at stake here was the 'object' or 'matter' or even the mere activity of philosophy, this would be of little account. The distinction that is being made here is, however, of a more serious order. To make distinctions in the order of knowledge is to make distinctions in the character and being of *what*, or rather *who* knows in the manner of what and how it is that they might know. The self-understanding that philosophy *is* and how that self understands itself in its world will be decisive also for the way in which the redemption in Christ will address it. In other words, what is at stake here is a certain orientation toward the human person.

Indeed, the 1983 Catholic Code of Canon Law makes most explicit the importance of philosophy: Canon §251, which deals with the formation of priests (and by implication – since this pertains to that area of formation which is directed towards growth in reflection on the things of faith – formation of Christian persons in general), states explicitly that philosophy both as a general discipline and in its history must be studied "that it might further the human formation [of the students], sharpen their mental acuity, so that they be more apt for theological study".[26] To undertake the task that philosophy is, is to undertake a certain deepening in self-understanding which is preparatory to, but not a substitute for, a deepening in the self's understanding of God.

Not that the redemptive action of God in Christ is *determined* by philosophy. What is at stake is the depth and complexity of how redemption will be received, and in being received, will itself be proclaimed anew by those who receive it in joy. A fear of philosophical over-determination, what Aristotle named as κατάφασις, or affirmation (which for Christians would be injurious to faith), neglects to remember that for Aristotle the effort of philosophy is also undertaken by way of denial. Denial is not negation: it is denial for the sake of bringing something better to light. In the production of false opinion, to say that so-and-so is not as it has been *falsely* said to be, is to open up again how it might be more truly experienced and so named. Ἀπόφασις belongs to κατάφασις, in the sense that the false is a mode of truth and not its binary opposite. The task of philosophy is to become proficient in

---

26 *Codex Iuris Canonici*, Vatican, Libreria Editrice Vaticana, 1983. §251: "ut ... formationem humanam perficiat, mentis aciem tradatur, eosque ad studia theologica peragenda aptiores reddat".

the ways of affirmation and denial that deepen the experience and sense of truth, so that when truth appears it can be better discerned.

My thesis is quite simple: the Papal tradition calls for the restoration of Aquinas because it judges that Aquinas is exemplary in the field of those who have shaped a theological understanding of faith through a profound and far-reaching philosophical reflection. The key term here is exemplary. It means that in appealing to Aquinas we are called to do what he does: to shape our own understanding of faith through a profound and far-reaching philosophical reflection – that will therefore take into account the self-reflection of those not yet received in faith. This is, after all, only what Aquinas did. To write *contra Gentiles* was to say: look how the philosophy you *already* know, now that it receives baptism, can feed you in the rich life of faith. To follow the Papal precept, and to imitate Aquinas – to do what he does – will mean that, taking into account what Aquinas himself said, we will speak differently from Aquinas. The consequence of this for the position I have outlined is that, no matter how seductive the results, an uncritical recapitulation of Aquinas will not do, because it will not speak to the heart of the age in which we live, and it will simultaneously distort and instrumentalise Aquinas himself. At its worst, for us, the repristinisation of Aquinas will reproduce that most postmodern of things, a theological theme-park, where we frolic, say, in the pastiche of a re-constructed and romantic castle, stunned by its prettiness, without ever remembering that castles were built to stabilise and defend the land, and subordinate the people of that land to social, economic, political and religious rule.

I want to return to Aquinas' reading of Aristotle, which I indicated had more far-reaching consequences than we have yet seen; consequences that Radical Orthodoxy has overlooked, and which are yet critical for any appropriation of Aquinas in modern theology. To illustrate why I believe my thesis to be correct, I want to appeal to one of the places where Aquinas most unites his philosophical understanding with his theology: the question of truth. He takes as his general orientation a selective interpretation of Aristotle's understanding of truth in the *Perihermeneias,* which he quotes specifically in the *Summa Theologiæ*: "According to the Philosopher, words are signs of intellections, and intellection is similitude to things".²⁷ Aquinas is already pressing in the direction of a particular interpretation of Aristotle, by equating intellection with εἶδος. (It needs to be noted that in the *Perihermeneias* Aristotle does not privilege εἶδος [ἤδη, the things that have a 'look'] over ὁμοιώματα, the things that are like to other things, and πράγματα, the things that are realities, which he also mentions.) This orientation is implicit, but just as governing in the *Quæstiones Disputatæ: de Veritate*.²⁸

Near the beginning of *de Veritate*, Aquinas asks: "Whether truth is found principally in the intellect or in things?".²⁹ He notes that the primary referent of truth is to the divine, not the human intellect. This is because he has already established that truth is an *adæquatio*, a correspondence of mind and thing.³⁰ The εἶδος, or picture, at issue resides both already, and primarily, in the divine mind: it is what the divine mind intends through having been its originating cause. This ensures that Aquinas does not get tangled by the problem of something being true in my mind even before I have come across it. For Aquinas, the 'correspondence theory of truth' has the happy effect that in my coming across any particular thing, the thing discovered will, through its truth, bring my intellect into conformity with the divine intellect. In knowing a thing I will in some limited sense share in the divine mind. Already we can see how the soteriology and respect for creation which is always at work in Aquinas is to be taken for granted in that most philosophical of concerns, the nature of truth.³¹

---

27  *Summa Theologiæ*, I, 1, q. 13, a. 1. "Secundum Philosophum, voces sunt signa intellectuum, et intellectus sunt rerum similitudines." Citing Aristotle Perihermeneias, I, 16a3. ὧν μέτοι ταῦτα σημεῖα πρώτος, ταὐτά πᾶσι παθήματα τῆς ψυχῆς, καὶ ὧν ταῦτα ὁμοιώματα, πράγματα ἤδη ταὐτά.

28  In many ways this early work is a more nuanced and complex work than either of the *Summæ*, being the fruit of actual disputations held in his first term as a *Magister* at the University of Paris.

29  Aquinas, *de Veritate*, Q. 1, a. 2, *Utrum veritas principalius inveniatur in intellectu quam in rebus.*

30  Aquinas, *de Veritate*, Q. 1, a. 1. "Prima ergo comparatio entis ad intellectum ut ens intellectui correspondeat: quæ quidem correspondentia, adæquatio rei et intellectus dicitur; et in hoc formaliter ratio veri perficitur."

31  It is worth noting that knowing the truth of a thing will not alone save me, but the point is that knowing its truth in this way potentially makes it available to point me toward where salvation is to be found. One of the problems with the Radical Orthodoxy position on truth in Aquinas is that it does not accomplish this distinction, precisely because it has not understood how Aquinas holds truth and salvation apart by also holding them together.

He accomplishes this conclusion by arguing that what is known "must be in the knower after the manner of the knower".[32]   If one of Thomas' orientations is from the *Perihermeneias*, the other, which he explicitly names in Question One of *de Veritate*, is Book VI of Aristotle's *Nicomachean Ethics*. Here, as Aquinas' commentary on this work confirms, Aristotle discerns five modes of how things may be true.   The first, ἐπιστήμη, Aquinas names as *scientia* and we would loosely translate as scientific knowledge of the natural world; the second is σοφία (*sapientia*), or wisdom: the highest philosophy. Science and wisdom are for Aristotle modes of truth about things that do not change, the ἀίδιον,[33] the things that always are the way they are.   The next two modes of truth are, τέχνη (*ars*) and φρόνησις, (*prudentia*).   These two latter relate to the things that undergo change: ἐνδεχόμενον ἄλλως ἔχειν.[34] As manners of being true, these four all relate to what I know, and are therefore modes which take place always together with and alongside the fifth way of being true, νοῦς, or knowledge, the 'truthfulness' of truth itself.

Aquinas however, selects only one of these five modes of truth for the determination of philosophical truth in *de Veritate*, and that is the mode of τέχνη.   In this, Aquinas' sheer genius is at work.   For Aristotle, τέχνη has a feature uncommon to any other of the modes of being true.   In the case of the other modes of being true the purpose of truth is for the sake of myself in contemplation: the εἶδος at issue is the result of the work (ἔργον) to be undertaken: it lies in the future, as what is to be striven for.   It is for this reason that each of these modes is referred by Aquinas to God's self-knowledge as Trinity, culminating in highest knowledge, which is wisdom (σοφία); hence God alone is truly wise in utterly perfect self-contemplation. However, in τέχνη the εἶδος, or 'look' that something takes always lies prior to it (in contrast to the other modes where it is in the future): the 'look' is the blueprint which must already exist, against which the thing to be produced must be measured to be true.   It is for this reason why Aquinas makes such a strong appeal to 'measure' in Question One of *de Veritate*, and why the mind

Knowing a truth will not save me, but knowing who made it true will.

32  Aquinas, *de Veritate*, Q. 1, a. 2, resp. "Oportet enim ut cognitum sit in cognoscente per modum cognoscentis."

33  Aristotle, *Nicomachean Ethics*, VI, 1139b23.

34  Cf. Aristotle, *Nicomachean Ethics*, VI, 1140a1.

is itself understood as measure in Question Ten.[35] The thing to be made is to be measured out according to the vision, or 'look' it has in the mind of the artificer.

Moreover, in τέχνη the οὐ ἕνεκα, the 'for the sake of which' something is produced, is specifically for the sake of something other than the artificer. The work done and its end (τέλος) result in a thing-produced: this house; that eclipse. Therefore, just as I can know something of the craftsperson in what he or she has crafted – precisely because the εἶδος of τέχνη is exteriorised as a creation (Aristotle says παρά, 'alongside', the one creating) *as* its very realisation in the artifice of the practice of the *ars*, so I can know something of God in knowing God's effects: creation itself, the *artificium divinum*, of which I myself am part.

Indeed, Aquinas makes direct appeal to how this is to be understood, comparing how all things are in the divine mind "as all artifacts find their origin in the mind of the artificer".[36] The others modes of being true fall into the background at this point, *precisely* because we know God philosophically through knowing creation, in the mode of knowing the results of God's τέχνη.

Because God can be known through creation, God can therefore be known without being known as Trinity. This distinction is essential for Aquinas, because he reserves the mode of truth given in τέχνη to philosophy alone. It is alone through this mode that God is known through something exterior to God, namely creation. It is for this reason he holds that the divine Trinity cannot be known by natural reason. The Trinity is truly known according to the properties by which the persons of the divine Trinity are distinguished. This knowledge requires faith, for it requires inclusion in the distinction, which mere knowledge *about* the Trinity (as, say, a non-believer might have through studying Christianity in a religious studies course) cannot give.[37] This distinction, between knowledge of God applied essentially to God (i.e. that

---

35 Aquinas, *de Veritate*, Q. 10, a. 1, resp. "Dicendum quod nomen mentis a mensurando est sumptum."

36 Aquinas, *de Veritate*, Q. 1, a. 2, resp. "Sicut omnia artificiata in intellectu artificis [sunt]."

37 Aquinas, *de Veritate*, Q. 10, a. 13 (*Utrum per Naturalem Rationem Possit Cognosci Trinitas Personarum* [*Whether the Trinity of Persons can be known by Natural Reason*], resp. "Dicendum, quod trinitas personarum dupliciter cognoscitur. Uno modo quantum ad propria, quibus distinguuntur personæ: et his cognitis, vere trinitas personarum cognoscitur in divinis. Alio modo ... hæc autem personis appropriata naturali cognitione cognosci possunt; propria vero personarum nequaquam."

God 'speaks'[38] or creates) through τέχνη, and knowledge of God as Trinity, is the basis for the fundamental distinction Aquinas makes in theology itself. Radical Orthodoxy is fond of treating the term 'theology' as a unitary term with a single meaning. In the *Summa Theologiæ*, however, at the very beginning, Aquinas says:

> Therefore theology which pertains to sacred doctrine differs in genus from that theology which is part of philosophy.[39]

The distinction operating here, which will later become the *theologia generalis* and *theologia specialis* taught by Baumgarten and understood by Kant, is already at work in Aquinas. Not only does Aquinas not conflate theology with philosophy, but he separates the theology at work in philosophy from the theology at work in that body of understanding concerning faith in God's revealing of himself, *Sacra Doctrina*, and he does this in virtue of an understanding of Aristotle's mode of truth in τέχνη.

It should be clear, however, that Aquinas' concentration on τέχνη protects the *un*knowability of God metaphysically and philosophically precisely because of a distinction he is making in the order of knowing of things. *Something* of the artificer is known through the artefact, but the artificer is more unknown than known. We do not know from Rothko's paintings what his favourite breakfast foods were. I would merely note that this takes place in Aquinas without any recourse to a doctrine of analogy, reinforcing the role analogy plays for faith and not philosophy. Indeed, the unknowability of God is demonstrated here *entirely* metaphysically and without recourse to anything which is even a *marker* for faith, which means that although the definition of truth that Aquinas is working with in *de Veritate* is entirely metaphysical, it is in no way injurious to faith. This is itself an important distinction because if metaphysics demonstrates (*probare*) the unknowability of God, it reserves to faith that it is precisely the order of knowing wherein God is known,

---

38  Aquinas, *de Veritate*, Q. 10, a. 13: ad. 10; resp. ad. 10.
39  *Summa Theologiæ*, I, 1, Q. 1, a. 1, ad. 2. "... unde theologia quæ ad sacram doctrinam pertinet, differt secundum genus ab illa theologia quae pars philosophiae ponitur." In the *Prologue* to Aquinas' commentary on Aristotle's *Metaphysics*, he similarly notes that "theology" can be the name of the science of the first substances: being, God, and the intelligences. It is clear that he is referring not to what is divinely, but what is naturally revealed. (Aquinas, *In Libros Metaphysicorum*, Prologus.)

because God is truly known only as Trinity, through the distinctions between the persons who have to be believed in before they can be really understood.[40]

Can I do the same? Can I propose an understanding of truth and knowing what is true which is the same as Aquinas' own? This is really Radical Orthodoxy's question, because it is the question of how Aquinas can be used and appealed to in contemporary theological thinking. I would answer in the following way. Aquinas has located truth primarily in the divine mind, secondarily in the human. He has located truth more in the divine mind than in things. By deft footwork he has produced an understanding of truth in which, nevertheless, things cause truth in us and not we in them,[41] still more deftly by privileging what for Aristotle was the least of the modes of being true, τέχνη. Now, in *de Veritate* he notes that even if there were no human intellects, there would still be truth, because of the prior relation of all things to the divine intellect. He then adds: "But if, by an impossible supposition, intellect did not exist and things remained, in no way would truth remain".[42]

Aquinas could conceive of a world in which there were no human intellects, but he could not have understood a world in which there were no intellection, or rather one where God was a dead thing: *quod est impossibile*. It is for this very reason that the schema of knowing things to be true that Aquinas takes over from Aristotle actually works. The intellection of God guarantees the re-ordering of Aristotle he has undertaken, and it guarantees truth overall.

Let me be quite clear about this. Aquinas says "even if there were no human intellects, things could be said to be true because of their relation to the divine intellect",[43] however, precisely the crisis of rationalism named by John Paul II (and by Radical Orthodoxy) has lead to the now universal assumption, formulated and crystallised by Nietzsche, that God is dead, which has precisely destroyed – devalued – the place of God as the guarantor of truth.

---

40  This is an entirely biblical concern: only the Son has perfect knowledge of the Father. (Cf. John 1[18]; 17[25])

41  Unless they are things we have actually fashioned for ourselves, in which case we are in the same relation to what we fashion as God is to God's creation. Cf. *de Veritate*, Q. 1 a. 2, resp.

42  Aquinas, *de Veritate*, Q. 1 a. 2, resp. "Sed si uterque intellectus, quod est impossibile, intelligeretur auferri, nullo modo veritas ratio remaneret."

43  Aquinas, *de Veritate*, Q. 1, a. 2, resp. "Unde, etiam si intellectus humanus non esset, adhuc res dicerentur veræ in ordine ad intellectum divinum."

If, as I argued in the *Radical Orthodoxy* volume, the divine intellect can no longer flatly be understood to be the guarantor of truth, precisely because the mode of knowing that is τέχνη has come to dominate in philosophy (exactly as Thomas privileged it) in a world where God is dead, and if it is precisely *that domination* which has given rise to nihilism, then exactly the situation which Aquinas asserts *impossibile est*, that things have remained whilst what most knows and intends them to be true has been carried off, then Aquinas' presupposition no longer holds that the other modes of being-true, ἐπιστήμη, φρόνησις, νοῦς, and the highest, σοφία, can be taken for granted. Worse still, the correspondence theory of truth will collapse – which modern philosophy is in many ways confronting.

Now why can we not, as Radical Orthodoxy seems to suggest (and Pickstock has reiterated in this volume), simply re-assert that God is the immediate guarantor of truth, an immediacy which we can also share, insofar as we share in bumpkinhood (which she suggested might be open to us, when she says "it seems that a token bumpkinhood is not denied us")?[44] Why does this *theological* understanding of truth not resolve all the contradictions into which 'philosophy' has fallen? Surely the very declarative faculty of Radical Orthodoxy, coupled with its skill in elegantly re-performing Aquinas permits such a clear re-assertion? In short, is not my criticism that Radical Orthodoxy lacks historical perspicacity its very strength?

If we just declare truth to be simple, and to be guaranteed by God – if we simply re-perform Aquinas' firmly held belief – surely the problem is solved, and nihilism is bracketed out? This is precisely the problem that Nietzsche foresaw. To re-assert God without paying attention to *why* the destruction of this particular understanding of the divine has come about is simply to create God anew. Following Aquinas directly here, such a God would be an artifice, *res artificialis*, who would be known only in the order of truth through τέχνη as something willed and produced, and asserted to be as God is *by us*: one whose prior created image would originate in the human mind making the assertion, not in the divine mind itself. It is here that Aquinas' notion of the mind as *measure* comes into its own. He says that insofar as we create artificial (i.e. not natural) things, we measure, exactly as God measures, by

---

44  See p. 72, and note 16, above.

creating.[45] Here it becomes clear how our minds are really analogous to God: not in cloddish bumpkinhood, but in the faculty of creativity itself. It is this very creativity which forces us to historical perspicacity, generally, and here in regard to Aquinas.

Now it becomes clear what the difficulty with the restoration of Aquinas is, why there can be no disingenuous restoration of his work in the present situation of philosophy. This does not mean that there can be *no* restoration of Aquinas. It means any restoration of Aquinas is going to have to explain why what for Aquinas *impossibile est* has become the prevailing understanding in what human being is. Any restoration of Aquinas is going to have to produce and elaborate a history of philosophy wherein Aquinas, and Aristotle for that matter, can be placed. It is going to have to explain our difference from them, and above all it will explain Aristotle differently *now* from the way Aquinas explained Aristotle *then* (precisely because it will have to re-appropriate the modes of being-true for philosophy that Aquinas takes for granted). It is, in short, going to have to undertake the work of explaining the being of being human anew, in order to deepen our acuity for theology. This means that, far from bracketing out 'modernity' or the Enlightenment, or whatever you want to name it, the hard work of historical perspicacity towards previous authors is going to have to explain that too. This hard work, of restoring thought through a respectful perspicacity towards texts and their authors, is itself not just a historical, but actually a philosophical task. Which is why philosophy, far from being evacuated and surpassed, has only just begun (and why, therefore, the Papal call is for the restoration, and not the evacuation, of philosophy). For these very reasons, what I have called the Radical Orthodoxy appropriation of Aquinas, however creatively re-presented, just won't do.

---

45 Aquinas, *de Veritate*, Q. 1, a. 2, resp. "Sic ergo intellectus divinus est mensurans non mensuratus; res autem naturalis, mensurans et mensurata; sed intellectus noster est mensuratus, non mensurans quidem res naturales, sed artificiales tantum."

# PART IV
# RADICAL ORTHODOXY
# AND THE QUESTION
# OF THE CONTEMPORARY

Chapter Seven

# Radical Orthodoxy
# and/as Cultural Politics

Graham Ward

Let me begin by raising a question of strict relevance to this paper: what makes a belief believable? Then let me rephrase that question as: what is involved in the production of believing? For, if Wittgenstein is right, reasoning has to give way to persuasion, since its possibility always lies upon unproven assumptions. So what persuades us? Belief arises, is called forth, when the evidence for what is true, the evidence for knowledge, is held on credit. Hence the link between credit, *credo* and credibility which always implicates economics in the practice of faith. Where the truth, value or meaning of something is not self-evident, we take on trust, or we entrust our judgement to accredited authorities who stand as guarantors for the truth, value or meaning of that which we have come to believe in. I employ 'we' because believing always involves relationships, even communities. One cannot believe alone for all believing opens up a space of or for a certain kind of activity and activity will necessitate, and be founded upon, the involvement of others.[1]

This belief suspends the certainties of present possession with respect to a future fulfilment. So when the vast national and now multi-national telecommunications giant British Telecom shouts to us from billboards up and down the country, and TV screens proclaim on its behalf everywhere in an entire nation that a thousand customers are returning to British Telecom every week, if I am to accept their claim then I must trust that someone somewhere does have immediate access to those statistics and will vouchsafe not only their existence, but that as statistics, they present real, not forged or

1   To take a Wittgensteinian line, just as there cannot be a private language so there cannot be a private belief.

manufactured data.  I have to trust also the laws governing advertising and such statutory bodies as the British Advertising Standards Council – who have been deputised by a British Act of Parliament to guarantee that no advert can blatantly lie to or mislead the public.

What I am suggesting here is that there is always an economics, a sociology and a politics of believing.  Let us pursue this further for a moment to develop something of the metaphysics of this economics, sociology and politics.  For you can hopefully see from my example how the examination of what makes a belief believable involves certain presuppositions about the way things are.  Let me draw three of these out.

First, believing requires  accepting the hard-core reality of some forms of legitimation.  As such believing is implicated in structures of authority: whether that authority is the expert, or the judge or the policeman or the government official, or the ecclesiastical official or the Scriptures.  But when even when we come to accept that legitimation, that authority in whom is deposited the true knowledge, if you like, we have to believe again in the legitimate operation of that legitimation.  For example, we have to believe that the Advertising Standards Council can indeed vouchsafe that we are not being mislead, because they have a superior knowledge to the general public; that the collector of statistics at British Telecom *can* verify that these figures accurately portray 1000 people who, each week, turn from mobile telephone providers like Orange or small, local telephone companies like UK Cambridge-based Ionica, say, back to British Telecom.  What, therefore, we are given to believe in that down payment, if you like, upon which we have to trust, is representative of the final truth, value or meaning which we are accrediting it with.  We have to accept what Derrida has recently termed the "promise of truth" implicit in all testimony.[2]

Secondly, believing involves presupposing the world is a certain shape; that there is a stable reality, a given open today to being digitally measured, digitally manipulated, and so 'known'.  If you like, believing, in our modern world, necessitates ontological foundations, whether empiricist or Platonic. Hence Christian theology since at least the sixteenth century has been

2   See Derrida, J., *Faith and Knowledge: The Two Sources of 'Religion' at the Limits of Reason Alone* in Derrida, J. and Vattimo, G., *Religion*, Cambridge: Polity Press, 1998, translated by Weber, S. (*La Religion: Séminaire de Capri sous la direction de Jacques Derrida et Gianni Vattimo*, Paris, Éditions du Seuil, 1996).

attempting to establish such ontological foundations which can ultimately treat God substantively. Witness Descartes' notion that the God with whom we have to do will not deceive us; which was Calvin's notion before it was Descartes'. Believing, in the modern world, involves processes of objectification, commodification. It involves not only the commodification of knowledge – 'this is true, that is false' – according to categories of identification, but that such atomistic handling of any given reality is *the* way to understand and grasp its truth. This implicates the need for legitimation and authority in certain intellectual power structures. Possessing knowledge, becoming the expert, is acquiring the power necessary to take up a position, begin a colonisation, start the process of domination.

Thirdly, believing involves presupposing that we can not only know what is but that we can communicate what is, represent it to ourselves and to others transparently. This comes back to a distinction I drew earlier with respect to legitimate agencies of knowledge, specific forms of testimony: to believe in their pronouncements involves accepting that they *can* represent the truth about what is.

'Representation' takes two forms here. Both forms are related to the facility to 'stand in for' that which is not immediately available to the rest of us. On the one hand, we are talking about the way certain institutions (and what are the politics at work dictating which institutions?) conduct themselves as representatives such that they are able to be first-hand knowers of the truth and therefore efficient media for the communication of that truth. On the other, we are talking about the means they have for that communication; the nature of communication itself. To believe, in our modern world, involves accepting that we can represent that world as it is: that the modes of communicating 'what is' are transparent. That is to say, to believe in the modern world involves accepting some construal of angelic knowledge. For the good angel is a messenger who seeks not to glorify himself or herself, seeks not to draw any attention away from the message he or she bears. The good angel is utterly consumed in the message; *is* the communication without remainder. Marshall McLuhan's famous dictum about late twentieth century communication – the medium is the message – is a secularisation of the knowledge possessed and communicated, possessed *as* communicated, by angels. Believing involves accepting the transparency and the innocency of narratives, performances of persuasion in which the medium melts into air in the process of announcing itself. Only in this way can things be as they are said to be.

I suggest there are three presuppositions then for modern believing: the belief in testimonial authority (authority can give an account of itself); the belief in foundational, demonstrable surety than can be atomistically accounted for; the belief in the transparency of representation. Believing is implicated, then, not only in an economics, sociology and politics, but also a metaphysics which organises the space opened up by the suspension of possessing the truth. It follows that if the economics, sociology, politics and the metaphysics cannot organise such a space then that which is offered as something to be believed in cannot be believed in – for the cultural space is not available. People will remain unpersuaded, or have to adapt what they are being offered to believe in to the spaces available for such a belief.

We could conceive this phenomenon in two ways: either, that beliefs come in and out of fashion, being subject to the same laws that govern the symbolic exchange or even flotation of signs, and implicated in announcing 'the myth of change'; or, that certain beliefs, like certain questions, are only available at certain times, as are also the means of understanding those beliefs or answering those questions.[3] That is, that just as the questions we ask today are the questions which today throws forward to be asked, and the methods we have for answering those questions evolve from the urgency of the question; so the beliefs we hold are the beliefs today throws forwards, and the methods for understanding those beliefs similarly take shape.

The difficulty is, that while modern believing requires we accept these three things – to wit: the belief in authority; the belief in foundational, demonstrable sureties than can be atomistically accounted for; and the belief in the transparency of representation – we are continually reminded, by the very mechanisms for gathering and evaluating evidence to substantiate belief, that authorities are ephemeral and open to challenge, that facts and the brutally given are plastic and malleable to interpretation, that representation (both institutional and discursive) involves distortion. Digits can only speak when decoded, and so statistics can never be absolved from casuistry sanctioned by

3   Baudrillard, J., *Symbolic Exchange and Death*, translated by Hamilton Grant, I., London, Sage Publications, 1993 (Baudrillard, J., *L'échange symbolique et la mort*, Paris, Gallimard, 1976), p. 90.

one body and policed by others. In other words, the critical reflection which facilitates modern believing also calls us to recognise crises of legitimation, crises of ontological foundationalism, and crises of representation. A gap opens up, and continues to open up exponentially, between *what* we are asked to trust in and *the means by which* we are being asked to trust in it. Credibility is being stretched towards incredulity.

Alert to this gap, the French critical theorist Michel de Certeau writes that what is constant in modern believing *is* the gap between "what authorities *articulate* and what is *understood* by them, between the communication they allow and the legitimacy they presuppose, between what they make possible and what makes them credible".[4] What ultimate authorities are there to guarantee the truth, value or meaning of the things we believe? Are they the social scientists, the natural scientists, the Government in power, the Pope, the Archbishops? And is their authority such that they can possess the certain knowledge of that which we hold on trust? Are they too not reading the newspapers, watching the television, listening to the debates and generally caught up the processes of coming to a belief about something themselves? Belief, it seems, demands a form of legitimation and a process of legitimation which is external to the immanent transactions and exchanges of believing. Belief demands surety; but there is only the endless circulations of information and interpretation. Our very believing rests upon a prior believing; reason gives way to persuasion.

De Certeau characterises the current ethos as a 'recited society': "Our society has become a recited society, in three senses; it is defined by *stories* (*récits*, the fables constituted by our advertising and informational media), by *citations* of stories, and by the interminable *recitation* of stories".[5] In a recited society people believe what they see and what they see is produced for them, hence simulacra-created belief: "the spectator-observer *knows* that they are merely 'semblances'... *but all the same* he assumes that these simulations are real".[6] This 'objectless credibility' is based upon citing the authority of others. Thus the production of a simulacrum involves making people believe that

4 De Certeau, M., *Culture in the Plural*, translated by Conley, T, Minneapolis, University of Minnesota Press, 1997 (*Culture au Pluriel*, Paris, Borgois, 1980), p. 15.
5 De Certeau, M., *The Practice of Everyday Life*, translated by Rendall, S., Berkeley, University of California Press, 1984 (*L'Invention du Quotidien: 1. Arts de faire*, Paris, Union Générale d'Éditions, 1980), p. 186.
6 De Certeau, M., *The Practice of Everyday Life*, p. 187 f.

others believe in it, but without providing any believable object. In a recited society there is a "multiplication of pseudo-believers" promoted by a culture of deferral and credit.[7]

In his account of our contemporary believing, de Certeau emphasises an aesthetics of absence. We are brought to believe in that which in itself is a representation of an object, not the object of belief itself. We defer the truth about the object to the testimony of other experts, whom we have never met nor can substantiate. These hidden experts in whom we put our trust enable us to accept as credible that which *we are told* is true. The space we as believers inhabit then is a space of "consumable fictions".[8] Caught up in the endless traffic and exchange of signs – from billboards, through television, in newspapers, on film, online – we construct from this seductive public rhetoric versions of 'reality' to which we give allegiance or in which we place our faith. These productions and exchanges organise what we take as our social reality. But since the flow of signs is constantly changing in the practices which make up everyday living, since ideas are constantly being modified, disseminated, re-experienced, re-expressed and transplanted, what is believable changes also. A continuous writing and rewriting of the stories of the true installs an aesthetics of absence.

This is what I mean by cultural politics, and all of us are caught up within the social energies generated and activated by it. We are implicated in the circulation and distribution of such energies, more so those of us who make public statements and are therefore involved in the plays of discursive power, disseminating our own narratives, offering our own bills of credit to which are appended our own cut-price offers, spaces for customer's signature, and squares for credit or debit card numbers. We are producing belief and reproducing that which we have come to believe. Theological discourse of whatever kind – sermons, books, articles in Academic Journals like *Modern Theology*, diary notes in the Parish magazine – is part of this endless circulation. There is no ideology-free zone. As such theological discourse requires to be examined as a cultural phenomenon by cultural studies. It needs to reflect upon itself. It too tells stories, narrates in order to persuade.

Now let us turn to the controversial issue of whether Christian theology does not just narrate but out-narrate; or what I have called Radical Orthodoxy

---

7    Blonsky, M. (ed.), *On Signs*, Oxford, Blackwell, 1985, p. 202.
8    De Certeau, M., *Culture in the Plural,* p. 25.

as cultural politics. I will proceed with two complimentary examinations: complimentary insofar as the two aspects of the Radical Orthodoxy project can only be separated *de jure*, not *de facto*. The first aspect I want to look at is Radical Orthodoxy's programme with respect to contemporary culture. And the second will be an examination of Radical Orthodoxy as itself a cultural production indissociable from that contemporary culture. In brief, first I will speak about Radical Orthodoxy as constructive cultural criticism and then about Radical Orthodoxy as a cultural product.

Christians are called upon, by Christ in the Gospel of Matthew most directly, to read the signs of the times. The Church is situated in an eschatological and soteriological management of time, established in its teachings on the Trinity and the relationship of the Triune God to Creation. Reading the signs of the times *is* the Church's participation in that management; Christians live in Christ and live pneumatologically through the practices of encountering, negotiating and interpreting the world around them. Those Christic and Pneumatic practices of everyday life are part of the in-gathering of all things into the Godhead. They draw creation's attention, not only to its radical contingency, but also, in and through that contingency, to its giftedness and its maintenance in grace.

It would seem to me that Radical Orthodoxy is involved in reading the signs of the times in such a way. It looks at 'sites' that we have invested much cultural capital in – the body, sexuality, relationships, desire, painting, music, the city, the natural, the political – and it reads them in terms of the grammar of the Christian faith; a grammar that might be summed up in the various creeds. In this way Radical Orthodoxy must view its own task as not only doing theology but being itself theological – participating in the redemption of Creation, by being engaged in the gathering of the differential *logoi* into the *Logos*. I will come back to this because it raises some of the issues of legitimation, power and representation I drew your attention to earlier.

For the moment, let me develop something of the 'radical' side of this enterprise. There are two aspects to this radicalism. First there is the rigorous rethinking of the Christian tradition and its significance for reading the modern world. Secondly, for me, the term *radical* is indissociable from certain left-wing connotations. In the collapse of socialism as a secular political force I see Radical Orthodoxy as offering one means whereby socialism can be returned to its Christian roots. Although socialism is fast dissolving into a Stakeholder society composed of contractual responsibilities (politics eclipsed by economics) one of the continuing effects of two centuries of socialist thinking has been its role in what the Frankfurt School called *Kulturkritik*. Critical theories from Benjamin and Habermas to Baudrillard and Šišek, that is to say, cultural studies itself, remains profoundly indebted to the ideology criticism that socialism fostered. I see Radical Orthodoxy as Christian *Kulturkritik* – and that, for me, means employing some of the tools furnished and honed by anthropologists and social and critical theorists to facilitate that Christian culture criticism. This is where some critics of Radical Orthodoxy, by presupposing a monolithic thesis held and implemented by all those associated with it, have pointed to difference between various contributors. As Gavin D'Costa recently states in a long review article on *Radical Orthodoxy*, "Blond seems entirely to write off postmodernity, while Ward is busily retrieving it".[9] I'm not sure this is what Phillip Blond is doing, but it seems evident to me that we cannot reject the cultural *Zeitgeist* that situates and contextualises us. The belief that we can is misguided and the attempt to do so gnostic.

To read the signs of the times means being aware of our involvement in them. Radical Orthodoxy is not about counter-culture. The counter-cultural mentality is apolitical, non-incarnational and operates in the province of sectarianism. Radical Orthodoxy's concern is with unmasking the cultural idols, providing genealogical accounts of the assumptions, politics and hidden metaphysics of specific secular varieties of knowledge – with respect to the constructive, therapeutic project of disseminating the Gospel. In this Radical Orthodoxy's *Kulturkritik* can move beyond the impasse of the Frankfurt School's negative dialectics, which deepened critique while becoming increasingly unable to believe the liberal, *Bildung* project: that consciousness-raising promotes liberation and social justice. The *Kulturkritik* of Radical Orthodoxy can accept the need for reflexivity, reject the harnessing of this to liberal humanism and inscribe its necessity, maintenance and direction in a Christian matrix, thereby practising a project governed by a soteriology; grounded in a Christian account of healing and redemption.

---

9   D'Costa, G., *Seeking after Theological Vision* (Review of *Radical Orthodoxy*) in *Reviews in Religion and Theology*, November 1999, Vol. 6, No. 4, p. 257; Blond, P, *Perception: From Modern Painting to the Vision in Christ* in *Radical Orthodoxy*, pp. 220-242.

Intrinsic to that project is re-establishing the necessary relationship between the secular world-view into the theological world-view from which it emerged as self-grounding, self-validating and atheistic. The secular cannot be secular without that theological framing which opens the space for its activity. Without the theological framing (and sanctioning), the secular space collapses in upon itself. It is the implosion of the secular that we are witnessing in the contemporary world. Various approaches to this task of re-establishing the theological order with respect to secularity and its immanent reasoning are discernible. There is John Milbank's critique of modernity and its social sciences – returning us to pre-modern accounts of the kingdom in Augustine, the Trinity in Gregory of Nyssa and the Christian metaphysics of Aquinas. There is Catherine Pickstock's critique of poststructural accounts of the sign, modernity's paradoxical necrophobia/necrophilia – returning us to the sacramental world of the pre-modern liturgy and the metaphysics of transubstantiation. There is Phillip Blond's critique of modernism, which seeks to overcome the nihilistic metaphysics he unmasks by returning us to theological accounts of perception.

My own work has increasingly focused on attempting to show how forms of postmodern thinking have re-enchanted the world and call for a theological reading – a reading which redeems them from the madness of semiosis and the endless deferral of the bad infinite.[10] That is, that the ethics and politics many of these thinkers are attempting to construct, the new incarnationalism many of them insist upon, is given a new, non-nihilistic coherence within a theological framework. If you like, the desires of postmodernism cannot be *post*-modern, contemporary post-secularism with its exaltation of the superficial, the kitsch, and the ephemeral, cannot be *post*-secular unless it is thought through on the basis of a theological grammar which has never accepted an autonomous secularity and allied itself with the modern to its detriment. As such, and as Lacan recognised, Augustine's theological account of the sign is a resource for the redemption of Saussure's differential

10  We can note here how the theses of several poststructural theorists have moved towards theological questions which they then either refuse to answer by way of invoking the death, or endless dissemination, of God. Take, for example, Jean Baudrillard's *Symbolic Exchange and Death*, (see note 3 above), which concludes with a chapter entitled *The Extermination of the Name of God*, or Jean-Luc Nancy's book, *La Communauté Désœuvrée*, Paris, Borgois, 1989, which concludes with a chapter on the names of the divine and the endless hæmorrhaging of their significance.

semiology; Gregory of Nyssa's account of *allegoresis* is a resource for the redemption of Derrida's and de Man's rhetorics of temporality; de Certeau's account of the lost body of Christ, which narrates a journey into endless exile, can be rethought, using de Certeau's concepts of space and tactics, into an account of the expansion of Christ's body such that all things find their place *in Christo*. If I have said more about my own project it is obviously because I know it better.

A certain Radical Orthodoxy principle remains throughout each of these projects – though there are differences too, for I emphasise, Radical Orthodoxy is not homogeneous. The principle, as I see it is this: employing the tools of critical reflexivity honed by continental thinking, taking on board the full implications of what has been termed the linguistic turn, Radical Orthodoxy reads the contemporary world through the Christian tradition, weaving it into the narrative of that tradition. And no, there is not *one* Christian tradition and yes we can speak to a certain extend about *orthodoxies*. For orthodoxy is broader than might at first be believed. It excludes only having first asked those challenging it to articulate fully the grammar of their beliefs. It is upon the grammar of their beliefs that it can be subsequently ascertained that they are not speaking according to the grammar of the church's faith. *Filioque* may divide, views on the Eucharist or even the sacraments more generally, may differ, but these are not grounds for heterodoxy. But if I claim that Jesus was a man adopted by God; if I claim that God is three people; if I claim the resurrection did not occur but that the disciples staged it – then I am no longer speaking the language of the Christian church. I am no longer in accord with the traditions of the faith that have been handed down to us.

And this is probably the best time to cross over from an account of what Radical Orthodoxy is attempting to produce to an account of Radical Orthodoxy as itself a cultural product of our times. For Radical Orthodoxy is involved in making its beliefs believable. It is attempting to clear that necessary space for believing in the present cultural matrix that I spoke of earlier. That its presence has attracted such widespread attention indicates that the space was available. But that means that Radical Orthodoxy is implicated in the cultural politics that organise such spaces. It cannot be naive about the three presuppositions of credibility which I outlined earlier. There is a reason why this theological project resonates in contemporary culture; why it creates fear and loathing in some quarters, is fêted in others, is welcomed, but with some suspicions and hesitations, in yet others. It is not being ignored and that is an indicator of its cultural significance.

Let me give two prominent examples of what is constructing certain cultural spaces at the moment. First, there is a general turn away from liberalism in First and Second World countries – those mostly affected by western civilisation. Fundamentalisms, neotribalisms, the constitution of imaginary communities, conservatisms – are high on academic and cultural studies' agenda at the moment. People elect to join these groups where they are offered a strong sense of identity and a system of shared values and priorities. We are increasingly becoming swipe-card carrying members of a whole host of clubs. I have heard someone describe Radical Orthodoxy as an elitist intellectual form of Christian fundamentalism. I was asked recently to defend Radical Orthodoxy against the view that it represented Christian, phallocentric imperialism. *Prima facie* Radical Orthodoxy as it is represented in that one opening volume *has* little to say for or by women. It has nothing to say about other theological practices of faith. Is it promoting (and I am not talking about individual intentions here, but public reception) Anglo-Catholic sectarianism?

These judgments, concerns and criticisms emerge as a consequence of the present cultural milieu. Let me put a distinctive Roman Catholic spin on this. The Dominican theologian Joseph DiNoia has noted in Catholicism a turn away from the *aggiornamento* mind-set that was in the ascendency up to and through the Vatican II Council: "there is a recovery of the astute insight that fuelled the work of the original *ressourcement* theologians: an uncompromising, unapologetic, but open affirmation of the fullness and richness of the Christian tradition".[11] He relates this to the cultural shift from modernity to postmodernity and observes it to be an aspect of postmodern theology. Editions of du Lubac are being reprinted; there are translations of Balthasar and Kasper's work in circulation. Furthermore, DiNoia links this turn to a change in the interpretation and reception of Aquinas. There is a connection for him between "a recovery of Aquinas ... and the refreshing postmodern agenda".[12] Because, he argues, postmodern culture revalues

---

11  DiNoia, J. A., *American Catholic Theology at Century's End: Postconciliar, Post-modern, and Post-Thomistic* in *The Thomist*, 1990, Vol. 54, No. 4.
12  DiNoia, J. A., *American Catholic Theology at Century's End*, p. 500.

participation, embodiment, temporal embeddedness, praxis and practical wisdom, and non-foundationalism then "Aquinas ... speaks with pristine clarity to a host of postmodern theological questions".[13] It is no accident that Radical Orthodoxy is having most of its public debates with and among Roman Catholics – take the conference which was the original pretext for this chapter, for example. And that the debate with Catholics has interpretations of Aquinas at its centre – take the middle section of this very book.

Not unrelated to the point I have just made, Radical Orthodoxy resonates within a cultural space that has been opened by a general cultural turn towards commodifications of nostalgia, most particularly new cultural investments in Mediævalism. In these cultural turnings, narratives of modernity are constructed, producing fables of modernity in which all our present calamities result from the aggressive consumerism and individualism of the early Renaissance, the repressive dualisms of Protestantism, and the universalisms of the Enlightenment. Radical Orthodoxy cannot be divorced from these trends. It did not invent the critical story of modernity it tells, but it does disseminate it – hopefully with more subtlety than some narrators – and its appeal to the pre-modern tradition can be viewed as peddling nostalgic palliatives. What is evident, then, is that Radical Orthodoxy is also historically and culturally embedded, and contingent. It is not a view from nowhere. It is not free of ideologies itself. Radical Orthodoxy also produces its beliefs within the cultural context of post-secularism and a new inflection of socialist thinking which has emerged as socialism as a political force finds no cultural space for the production of belief.

Radical Orthodoxy needs to reflect theologically upon the situatedness of its own 'knowledge'. It too is a sign of the times which requires reading. It is also produced, and so we need to ask "who is speaking and for whom and on whose authority?" Hence the questions about the ecclesial basis of Radical Orthodoxy – so fundamental to a project working with construals of the tradition and Christian praxis – cannot be shied away from. Likewise questions concerning the nature of our claims (are they ontological or rhetorical or is the distinction between the ontological and the rhetorical a construct of modernity anyway that can be sublated theologically?). We need to examine the extent to which it is itself the product of modernity, perpetuating the dualisms it is seeking to overcome. Are we sufficiently

13 DiNoia, J. A., *American Catholic Theology at Century's End*, p. 511.

postmodern? We need to examine the stories we construct – for genealogies are stories (Foucault called them *récits*, de Certeau *fables*, Serres, *légende*). One of the characteristics of Radical Orthodoxy is its concern with cultural context, its reflections on time and embodiment, and its commitment to historicism. But this commitment to aspects of historical contingency has a critical feedback: whose Augustine are we trafficking, whose Gregory, whose Aquinas? That is not to say there cannot be worse or better readings of the work of these theologians, only that we have learnt too much about hermeneutics, from the work of Hans-Georg Gadamer in particular, not to be conscious of the way we make the past in our own image, through our own cultural demands. Radical Orthodoxy is involved in the production of belief, the making of sense, the composition of a discursive body.

We need to attempt to relate how the discursive body it produces corresponds not only to the body of Christ – the Eucharistic body, ecclesial body and Trinitarian activity – but the social and political bodies that organise and disseminate internalised cultural values. Furthermore, and as a corollary of this, those of us involved with Radical Orthodoxy must attempt to give not only a theological account of time, but a theological account of history if we are to understand our own genealogical method theologically. We can all too easily slip into constructing a historical demon (Scotus, Ockham, Suárez, Kant, might all be offered as candidates) in order to make the angel of peace more prominent. We always need to handle subtle and sophisticated accounts of modernity's engagements. We have to ask whether anything good has come out of secularism? Was the world not sustained by God throughout modernity? Can theology only proceed on the basis of constructing the errors and heresies of past theologies and demonising them? Is it not rather that the questions we are asking today are not the questions Tillich asked, or Barth, or Luther, or Suárez, or Ockham? Is there not a need for an account of the theological task and the Christian tradition, an account *of* orthodoxy and orthodoxies? And what about those other forms of orthodoxy and orthodoxies in Judaism and Islam? If the 'radical' in Radical Orthodoxy is not to conjure up connotations of separatism and sectarianism, then we will have to think through this production of belief with respect to the practices of other faiths, the devotions, prayers and offerings of other worshippers.

The questions Radical Orthodoxy must address pile up. There is work to be done. But it strikes me that is the most exciting aspect of the project: the sense of there being a theological task in a secular world; a theological task which is not just Christianity's; a theological task called forth by the way certain postmodern figures have been using and quoting theological language and terms, speaking at the end of scientism about spirituality and incarnation. Theological questions are permeating into the public domain. It is this which calls forth a specific theological task for today, which demands the difficult conceptual and scholarly work to be undertaken in order to address, rather than accommodate or be marginalised by, post-secularism, late capitalism, the hyperrealisms, the cyberspaces, the gnosticisms and the *faux* mysticisms of postmodernity.

Let me return to my analysis of what constitutes believing at the beginning of this essay, and draw a specific conclusion. As with all believing, Radical Orthodoxy is bound to reflect upon questions concerning the politics and rhetorics of its own practices. It is producing a belief. Nevertheless, the belief it is producing is not the same kind of 'consumable fictions' that create de Certeau's "pseudo-believers". It is not believing either without belonging – for commitment to specific ecclesial communities is the beginning and end of its reflections. Neither is it believing without substance. This returns us to that question I posed between making an ontological claim, 'this is the truth', and being engaged in a rhetoric of persuasion, what John Milbank in *Theology and Social Theory* termed "outnarrating".

Viewed as simply a rhetorical practice producing a Christian set of beliefs then Radical Orthodoxy would be doing no more than British Telecom – and would have to compete for punters in exactly the same way. It would be peddling nostalgia to those wishing to adhere to a tradition. It would be a theological adjunct of the current heritage industry. But the believing we are engaged in is not just produced. It is promulgated. For the believing and the proclamation of that believing arises from and must always return to the church's ontological claim that this is the truth; a claim based upon the church as the recipient and mediator of the revelation of Christ. That truth is not available as a commodity. Therefore theological assertions based upon that truth must always be aware of the fragility of being human; the social, political and economic matrix from which it emerges. It must always recognise the need for what Donald MacKinnon termed a healthy agnosticism. Augustine comes to mind, the Augustine who stood at the threshold of a coming Christendom in parallel fashion, perhaps, to us who stand at the end of Christendom, and says: "ignorance is unavoidable – and yet the exigences of human society make judgement also unavoidable".[14] The dialectic between ontological claims and the rhetoric of persuasion opens up an endless questioning within which faith seeks understanding. Radical Orthodoxy must view itself both as speaking to and speaking from a cultural politics.

14  Augustine, *de Civitate*, Book XIX, Ch. 6.

# Chapter Eight

# Revelation and the Politics of Culture
# A Critical Assessment
# of the Theology of John Milbank

Oliver Davies

It is a primary task of theology in every age to rethink the object of faith, which by faith we hold to be eternal, and to do so in terms which are authentically contemporary – and therefore contingent. Paradoxically only in this way can revelation be truly revealed, expressed in a living tradition that is rooted in the evolving realities of time and space. If theologians reject this task, or pursue it only half-heartedly, they run the risk that theology itself will become a mere cultural form. Then tradition will cease to be a living thing, dynamically of the present, and will simply represent a debt to the past. To this extent, theology is in a real sense subject to its continuing dialogue with philosophical thought, and therefore tends to share the structure of its evolution. This can be characterised as advance by radical revolution, whereby a single original thinker presents a complex of new concepts and understandings which abruptly supersede what has gone before, while taking many years to assimilate fully and to refine.

We are currently experiencing just such a theological accommodation of a critical philosophical breakthrough, which can be summarised as 'the linguistic turn' or the rise of what Voloshinov called "the philosophy of the sign". Although Wittgenstein is clearly an important figure in this, as are the later Martin Heidegger, Charles Pierce and Jacques Derrida, we cannot pin this movement on any one figure or philosophical grouping. The turn to the sign is too pervasive in many dimensions of contemporary thought for this, in what can be seen as a near universal rejection of essentialism. Indeed, language itself has come to occupy the central place previously held by metaphysics, and linguistic theory, or defining what language is, plays the role of ontology in earlier centuries. In other words, the way we grasp language governs our understanding of self, other and world. But in this period of theological realignment following the turn to language, the same fundamental problematic arises which we have seen time and again in theological history, and the answer to which itself constitutes in no small degree the nature of the theology that is done. Where do the boundaries lie between revelation of the eternal and the contingency of philosophical thought? How can we ensure that philosophy serves theology and does not become its master?

John Milbank belongs to a younger generation of theologians whose work represents the re-figuring of tradition in the light of perspectives which belong to the new scepticism of the 'postmodern' movement in philosophy.[1] As such, he represents a late, if not a final, stage of response in that certain features of the 'postmodern', most notably 'incommensurability' and the primacy of language as 'writing', are taken not as being revolutionary but rather as axiomatic. Indeed, in *The Word Made Strange* Milbank undertakes a re-reading of "the linguistic turn, not as a secular phenomenon, but rather as the delayed achievement of the Christian critique of both the *antique form* of materialism, and the antique metaphysics of substance".[2] Thus it is in Louth, Vico, Hamann, and Herder that we see the "real achievement of a non-instrumental and metaphorical conception of language" as "part of an ultimately theological and anti-materialist strategy".[3] Furthermore, the deconstruction of Jacques Derrida actually remains tied to a residual Platonism in Milbank's view so that "only Christian theology, as the conception of a non-violent *semiosis*, is truly 'without substance'".[4]

Indeed, although theology and "sceptical postmodernism" alike have been able "to think unlimited semiosis", it is only for theology that "difference remains real difference since it is not subordinate to immanent univocal process or the fate of a necessary suppression" but is "a peaceful affirmation of the other, consummated in a transcendent infinity".[5]

---

1   Here there is a contrast with the work of Mark C. Taylor, for instance, in whose *Erring: A Postmodern A/theology*, London, University of Chicago Press, 1984, deconstruction has a revolutionary force.
2   Milbank, J., *The Word Made Strange*, Oxford, Blackwell, 1997, p. 97.
3   Milbank, J., *The Word Made Strange*, p. 106.
4   Milbank, J., *The Word Made Strange*, pp. 61 and 85.
5   Milbank, J., *The Word Made Strange*, p. 113.

Here then we find in outline Milbank's argument that deconstruction is fundamentally a Christian phenomenon, and that it is only Christianity which can bring the radicality of deconstruction to perfection.  The failure to understand the sacred origins of deconstruction leads to nihilism, while the drawing out of the Trinitarian foundations of deconstruction marks the return of a dynamic and theophanic Christian world-view.  By proposing his Christian "metasemiosis", Milbank succeeds both in contesting the autonomy of contemporary secularism and in creating a strikingly original re-narration of the Christian story.  But this considerable achievement is gained at a cost, for there is a repeated tendency to link Christian faith with particular philosophical positions, which naturally raises the old question of the boundary between faith and philosophy in a new and provocative way. It may be that the imaginative, though contested, reading of historical sources which Milbank undertakes serves, from one perspective, to overcome the nihilism of secular discourse by a Trinitarian 'metasemiosis'; while, from another, it can appear to import into Christian theology the very secularism to which Milbank's own Christian rhetoric remains vehemently opposed.

John Milbank's uncritical presupposition that there is an irreducible opposition between radicalised semiological difference on the one hand and a stubbornly Aristotelian-Cartesian view of 'substance' on the other, is one such philosophical commitment.  This stark and polemical polarisation is already present in Nietzsche, reappearing in Derrida and Deleuze, and it significantly slants Milbank's rendering of the tradition.  There can be no mediations between 'substance' (Aristotle) and 'relation' (semiosis), and so such a determinedly ontological thinker as Thomas Aquinas is elided into semiosis on account of his theory of participation, which "would be commensurate with a reality of shifting identities, composed solely of relative figural differences and affinities".[6] A second philosophical importation is that of the incommensurability of narratives.  The question of the 'incommensurability' of conceptual systems is a theme that has engaged a number of critical thinkers, including W. V. Quine and Donald Davidson, who have linked it with problematics to do with 'untranslatability', relativism and

6    Milbank, J., *The Word Made Strange*, p. 111.

truth-criteria.[7]    For Alisdair MacIntyre, incommensurability is to a considerable degree a condition of language-constituted traditions, but in *Whose Justice? Which Rationality?* he argues that a hegemonic tradition must have sufficient common ground with others to allow the occurrence of what he calls an "epistemological crisis" which permits a readjustment or a reaffirmation of the truth claims of that tradition in the light of those of alternative systems.[8] The vitality and hence hegemony of major traditions actually depend upon such a repeated process of correction and revaluation.[9]

Milbank dismisses MacIntyre's moderate incommensurability however on the grounds that it represents the triumph of "dialectics" over "narrative" and shows MacIntyre's indebtedness to the Enlightenment tradition. Against the mediations of reason underlying MacIntyre's corrective interactions across traditions, Milbank argues that "what triumphs is simply the persuasive power of a new narrative".[10] His own version of "radical incommensurability" is exemplified in the assertion that there can be no place for realism since, for the Christian, there can be no way of viewing the world except as "an evaluative reading of its signs as *clues to ultimate meanings and causes*": "thus the Christian grasp of reality *right from the start* is utterly at variance with anything the world supposes to be 'realistic'".[11] While we recognise the ultimate and totalising claims of Christianity as a way of appropriating 'reality', there is more at play here than the thrust of absolute metaphysical affirmations.

The phenomenon of 'reality' itself is complex, and human experience entails the interweaving of different orders of belief, some personal, some

7   W. V. Quine summarises his influential idea of "radical translation", showing the "indeterminacy of translation" and "indeterminacy of reference" in his *Pursuit of Truth*, Massachusetts, Harvard University Press, 1990, especially pp. 37-59. Davidson, D., in *On the Very Idea of a Conceptual System* in *Inquiries into Truth and Interpretation*, Oxford, Oxford University Press, 1984, pp. 183-198, develops Quine's position in order to attack the notion both of relativism and "the concept of an uninterpreted reality", since "if we cannot intelligibly say that schemes are different, neither can we intelligibly say that they are one" (p. 198).

8   MacIntyre, A., *Whose Justice? Which Rationality?*, London, Duckworth, 1988, pp.361-369.

9   "Only those whose tradition allows for the possibility of its hegemony being put in question have rational warrant for asserting such a hegemony" (MacIntyre, A., *Whose Justice? Which Rationality?*, p. 388).

10  Milbank, J., *Theology and Social Theory. Beyond Secular Reason*, Oxford, Blackwell, 1990, pp. 339-347.

11  Milbank, J., *The Word Made* Strange, p. 244.

cultural, some imaginative, some religious, and some which, in the modern world, are tied to what Quine calls "observation sentences" and their ramifications in empirical science. For all our caution about scientism, we are not at liberty to contest factors such as the speed of light, or the structure of DNA, at will. 'Reality' is necessarily constructed from a variety of narrative sources, some of which are scientific, and thus social and shared. By revaluing 'truth' as 'persuasiveness', Milbank is in effect advocating a robustly relativist view: "we should only be convinced by rhetoric where it persuades us of the truth, but on the other hand truth *is* what is persuasive, namely what attracts and does not compel".[12] The advocacy of relativism is notoriously difficult however, and Milbank seems to shun this task by straightforwardly asserting – through his historical readings – the identity of a post-Enlightenment understanding of truth as persuasion with specifically Christian modes of thought. This is tantamount to deconstruction *de fide*. But for all its brilliant simplicity, it is a strategy which has significant philosophical and theological consequences that are in conflict with the very narrative Milbank is seeking to propagate, as an "ontology of peace". Incommensurability licenses a polemical and oppositional view of narrativity, setting the Christian story over and against alternative narratives. This might seem to preclude the more 'peaceful' strategy of advocating the Christian narrative as the site in which other narratives find their true meaning.

Next, it disconcertingly serves also to align Christianity as an exercise in 'persuasiveness' with other rhetorics, which can equally point to their power to persuade which, in Milbank's terms, must be taken as evidence of their 'truth' (indeed, one of the problematics for the Christian community today is precisely the failure of its narrative to 'persuade' so many in contemporary society). How are we to distinguish between Gospel and ideology if conversion is the sole or chief criterion? And how are we to judge whether conversion is deeper than the rehearsal of a narrative which in some societies has been a near universal form of cultural practice? Further, rhetoric and persuasion are themselves consummately manifestations of privilege and power. Rhetoric, as advertising and as political campaigning, is about social manipulation and control, undertaken in the interests of elite groups. Although there are also important rhetorics of asceticism, liberation and detachment within our society, the uncritical alignment of Christianity and

12  Milbank, J., *The Word Made* Strange, p. 250.

ideology through the epistemology of bare-fisted rhetoric will inevitably pose the question of whether the uncritical alliance of Christianity and "radical incommensurability" might not result precisely from a failure to interrogate the philosophical underpinnings of Radical Orthodoxy in the light of the non-coercive and empowering dispositions of the Gospel.

Most importantly, Milbank follows a particular understanding of the nature of language which derives in the main from Derrida, whose philosophy of *différance* Milbank has hospitably recognised as an important anticipation of the Christian Trinitarian metasemiosis (albeit one which is in itself nihilistic). This understands language to be essentially 'writing', radically separated from conversation in which embodied speech agents openly and dialogically engage with each other in the collaborative weaving of text.[13] As we indicated above, lingocentrism in one form or another has effectively taken the place of metaphysics, resulting in the emergence of what we might term 'linguistic cosmology'. According to this view, language is not a tool or a medium used by agents negotiating world, but itself constitutes reality in such a way that 'subjectivity' and 'world' becomes functions of language itself. It is language that is the given, and the speaker becomes an epiphenomenon of the spoken.

While we welcome the insight into the centrality of language that this "hermeneutical ontology" (as Vattimo calls it) entails, we regret its failure to accommodate non-linguistic forms of experience (such as a shared realm of sentience) and, in parallel with this, its neglect of the dynamic actuality or sociality of language, grounded in speech between individuals (or conversation), which underlines its intrinsically *dialogical* character. It is precisely this view of language which is supported not only by advocates of dialogism such as Mikhail Bakhtin, Paul Ricœur, and Emmanuel Levinas, but pragmatic theory of this kind has also become the dominant school of language theory, strongly affirming the conversational word, in its actual social context, as the primary site of language. This is to emphasise 'contextual meaning' or 'meaning in interaction'.[14] In our conclusion we shall

13 Derrida, J., *De la Grammatologie*, Paris, Éditions de Minuit, 1967, especially pp. 42-108. (Translated by Spivak, G. C. as *Of Grammatology*, London, John Hopkins University Press, 1974, pp. 27-73.)

14 See, for instance, Yule, G., *Pragmatics*, Oxford, Oxford University Press, 1996, p. 3 and Thomas, J., *Meaning in Interaction*, London, Longman, 1995. The origins of pragmatics can be traced back to linguistic anthropology on the one hand, specifically the work of Malinowski and J. R. Firth, which set out the social contexts of speech, and to semiotics

advance ways in which pragmatic theory resonates positively with Christian revelation.

The Christian transformation of 'hermeneutical ontology' has led Radically Orthodox authors to advocate analogy and a semiotics of participation as part of a project to inaugurate the return of a Mediæval world-view. The re-performance of Mediæval tradition, often splendidly achieved, is the key to a metanoia generated by the multiple surfaces of a speech made strange, repristinised, and, by creative alienation, re-ordered to its origins in divine excess. The human person, as subject of praise, is encoded within language in such a way that linguistic repristinisation is simultaneously personal reformation – in Augustine's sense – into the order of praise and glory. The subject, exposed to the abyss of nihilism by secularism, is now retrieved as suppressed subject in the δοξάζω without whose presence, though inscribed merely as a suffix *within* the verb, the word itself would have no meaning. A theophanic understanding of language, rooted in a Trinitarian metaphysics, is indeed an ancient Christian idea. But the difficulties with the reintroduction of such a tradition in the modern world lie in the cosmological claims of the Mediæval tradition, and their incompatibility with a modern world view. This becomes evident in an analysis of texts by Meister Eckhart, for instance, who – as a late Mediæval German Dominican – inherited both a highly Platonic understanding of language, mediated through Augustine, and the particular commitment to proclamation which characterises the spirituality of the *Ordo Prædicatorum*. The recent requirement to preach in the vernacular, with all

on the other (Firth, J. R., *The Tongues of Men*, London, Watts & Co., 1937). In addition to foundational work by the American anthropologists Sapir and Whorff, and by the philosophers Charles Peirce and Ludwig Wittgenstein, all of whom stressed the centrality of language in the construction of social and cognitive realities, speech-act theory as developed by Austin, J. L., *How to do Things with Words*, Oxford, Oxford University Press, 1962, and later by Searle, J., *Speech Acts*, Cambridge, Cambridge University Press, 1969, also drew out the social and contextual aspects of language. This new movement was in reaction to Bertrand Russell's view of ordinary language use as debased communication from the perspective of a strict logical coherence, and it stressed the effective communication between speakers in their social environments and the extent to which speech is not tied to reference but is commensurate with action. In 1967, Paul Wátzlawick, Janet Beavin and Don Jackson published their *Pragmatics of Human Communication: a Study of Interactional Patterns, Pathologies, and Paradoxes*, London, Faber, 1968, lending added popularity to the term (see Aubrey Fisher, B., and Adams, K. L., *Interpersonal Communication: Pragmatics of Human Relationships* (second edition), New York, McGraw-Hill, 1994, p. 4).

the challenge of creating a new linguistic medium for the proclamation of the Gospel, can only have heightened the sense of the sacred character of the word preached.[15]

There are two dimensions to Eckhart's reflections upon the word, or image (*daz bild*). The first derives from a Neoplatonic metaphysics of the αρχή or *principium*, whereby what proceeds from its principle remains within it. As he states in Sermon 16a, drawing upon the figure of the mirror: "The image is not of the mirror, and it is not of itself, but this image is most of all *in* him from whom it takes its being and its nature".[16] The second is a theology of the creation, which understands the transcendentals to remain *within* God. Eckhart explicitly rejected a Thomist understanding of analogy, whereby the creation is related to the Creator as an effect to a cause and is ranked below the Creator, and advocated instead a form of analogy which maintains that the property of the first analogate does not properly belong to the second analogate but inheres in it only by imputation. This applies to every perfection, including existence.[17]

In the *Commentary on John*, Eckhart combines Nicene theology with philosophical notions to do with the relation of an image to its origin, and with analogy. He argues that if the Son is of one essence with the Father, though different in person, then the just man is the "offspring" (*proles*) of justice, and is one essence with justice, though different in person.[18] It is against the background of this kind of theory that Eckhart reflects upon the nature of the image in general and of the image of God in us, as 'intellect', in particular. The highest kind of image is the 'word', which proceeds from its *principium*

---

15  It is notable for instance that Mechthild von Magdeburg and Julian of Norwich, who are among the earliest spiritual writers in the vernacular, both have high theories of inspiration. See Davies, O., *Transformational Processes in the Work of Julian of Norwich and Mechthild of Magdeburg* in Glasscoe, M. (ed.), *The Medieval Mystical Tradition in England*, Vol. V, Cambridge, D. S. Brewer, 1992, pp. 39-52.

16  *Meister Eckhart: Die deutschen und lateinischen Werke: Herausgegeben im Auftrage der Deutschen Forschungsgemeinschaft*, Stuttgart and Berlin, W. Kohlhammer Verlag, 1936–, *Deutsche Werke*, Vol. I, translated by Davies, O., in *Meister Eckhart: Selected Writings*, Harmondsworth, Penguin Books, 1994, p. 192. ( My emphasis.)

17  *Meister Eckhart: Die deutschen und lateinischen Werke, Lateinische Werke*, Vol. II, p. 282.

18  According to Eckhart's neoplatonist metaphysics, the creature is essentially distinguished from the Creator on the grounds that the mode of existence of creatures is pluriform, whereas God is perfect unicity. In other words, the properties which are still rooted in the divine coexist in the creature in a state of multiplicity whereas in God they are wholly united within his divine unity.

through an act of intellection, and it is this mechanism which is at work both in the generation of the Son from the Father and the emergence of words from the human mind, since both events are governed by the dynamic of intellection. Eckhart is thus able to link language and Christology, declaring "daz wort kommt von dem worte": "all words come from the word".[19] Now language itself becomes theophanic. All that is required is that language should subject itself to a process of ascesis, or what Joseph Quint called *Entkonkretisierung.*[20] By shedding any reference to the world of fallen, created and multiple forms, language can be restored to its primal, unified and divine nature.

Thus, for Eckhart the preacher, purified and repristinised language, or what he calls "the eternal word", can actually make God present for those who listen (present that is in the particular sense which presence carries for Eckhart, as a presence-absence, as long-far). This is a true linguistic sacramentalism therefore which fosters Eckhart's own very particular kind of transformative rhetoric.[21]

Here then we find all the elements of Milbank's enchanted universe, with language at its centre, as participatory image of the Trinitarian fecundity. Here all is ordered to the divine. But there are important distinctions. Eckhart is not offering his listeners an alternative world-view to the prosaic materialism of his day. He is presenting them with what he understands to be a 'scientific' account of the creation of the world, and of the nature of language. If we wish to re-enact today the God-centredness of Eckhart's language theory, then we are confronted with a stark choice. Either we must embrace the 'science' which underlies it or we must jettison his theory of the divine provenance of language while holding to the principle that language can and must be ordered mystagogically to the divine reality. If we do the former, then we alienate ourselves from the modern world. Eckhart makes no

---

19  Sermon 18 (*Meister Eckhart: Die deutschen und lateinischen Werke, Deutsche Werke,* Vol. I, pp. 499-501).

20  Quint, J., *Die Sprache Meister Eckharts als Ausdruck seiner mystischen Geisteswelt* in *Deutsche Vierteljahrsschrift für Literaturwissenschaft und Geistesgeschichte,* 1928, pp. 671-701 (here 685).

21  I have argued for the centrality of this sermon for an understanding of Eckhart's otherwise suppressed language theory in Steer, G., and Sturlese, L., eds., *Lectura Eckhardi. Predigten Meister Eckharts von Fachgelehrten gelesen und gedeutet,* Stuttgart, Verlag W. Kohlhammer, 1998, pp. 98-115.

distinctions whatsoever between what is known by faith and what is known by reason, between physics and metaphysics, and 'science' for him is what can be reasonably demonstrated from the authoritative statements of the Bible, the Fathers and select classical philosophers.[22] Science for us, on the other hand, is what can be shown to be empirically the case (not even a radical relativist would wish to deny that the earth orbits the sun: a proposition which Eckhart's 'science' would have compelled him vehemently to deny).

But if we jettison the Mediæval cosmology which underlies Eckhart's system of participation, then we appear to want the fruits of a Mediæval world-view without buying into the fourteenth century physics which supported it. That is to re-enact the divine substantialisms of the Mediæval systems within the purely linguistic medium of current theological perspectives and debate. In other words, it is to exchange a Mediæval pseudo-scientific cosmic realism which supports a view of language as enchantment, for a purely rhetorical cosmos which understands enchantment to be a factor of language. The extra-linguistic world of the Mediævals, which constituted for them the cosmos, in all its theophanic hierarchy, and which served also to sustain and contain language in its realisations as doxology, has now become a potentiality within language itself: as rhetoric, rhetoric of the sublime.

John Milbank's reworking of 'hermeneutical ontology' or what we have called 'linguistic cosmology' reflects a highly perceptive insight. Cosmology – or the lack of it – is in many ways the fundamental issue of our modern religious situation. The Christianity we inherit came into existence within the context of an integral cosmology, which it still presupposes in all kinds of ways. But contemporary cosmological thinking has been formed by other sources. We will mean various things when we confess the name of God as creator, but there are not many of us today who regard the creation account in Genesis as literal truth, any other account as dangerous fiction, and for whom such a belief in no way compromises our rationality. Rationality for us will insist upon a causal account of the nature of the world drawn from the natural

---

22  One of the chief characteristics of Eckhart's work, as a German Dominican, is the tendency to combine philosophical and theological positions in a comprehensive understanding of the unity of truth: "all that is true, whether in knowledge, in Scripture or in nature, flows from a single fount, a single root", so that "the teachings of the holy Christian faith, and the writings of both Testaments are to be understood with the help of the natural reasonings of the philosophers". (*Meister Eckhart: Die deutschen und lateinischen Werke, Lateinische Werke*, Vol. III, p. 4 f.)

sciences to be maintained together perhaps with a religious account of the *meaning* of the world. What we cannot do then is hold Mediæval beliefs about the world *in the way that the Mediævals held them*. Once what we know as scientific reasoning has intervened, it cannot be unthought. The unravelling of the Mediæval cosmos had the further effect of denuding the self.[23] In the Mediæval universe, the cognitive faculties of the self were ordered towards God on account of the objective nature of the world he created, and of which we are a part. But with the empirical turn in philosophy, which took place across a period of centuries, they came to be seen as ordered to the material dimensionality of empirical reality. With the loss of a theistic cosmology, the affirmation of the existence of God entailed constructing at every step what it might mean for our purely secularised cognitive faculties to 'know' God. It is also the loss of cosmology then that underlies the rise of theological anthropologies in the late eighteenth and early nineteenth centuries.

All too easily we associate this trend with Schleiermacher and the use of the human as a measure of the divine, but there were numerous powerful theological systems which built creatively upon forms of idealism, as we find in the work of Anton Günter, for instance, or Johann Sebastian Drey. Theological anthropology surely is a tacit recognition of the cosmological problem and an attempt to reinstitute Christian cosmology by modelling the human person in such a way that he or she could only belong in a theistic universe. Rather than reading the self theologically as part of a Christian cosmos, as the Mediævals did, post-Mediæval theological anthropology is the attempt to read the universe theologically on the grounds of the human person.

It is likewise the human person – understood in a certain way – who stands at the heart of John Milbank's project. Milbank argues for an understanding of humanity as "fundamentally poetic being". He rightly makes a plea for "a Christian ontology which does justice to culture and history as an *integral* element of Christian being alongside contemplation and ethical behaviour, rather than as a 'problem' external to faith".[24] Poeticity is the human capacity to construct meanings, which as a form of creativity, aligns humanity with the

23  The traumatic and pivotal desacralisation of cosmology has recently been usefully traced in Randles, W. G. L., *The Unmaking of the Medieval Christian Cosmos, 1500-1760*, Aldershot, Ashgate, 1999.

24  Milbank, J., *The Word Made Strange*, p. 79.

divine *ars* of the *verbum*. As we have seen, Milbank views the rise of the philosophy of the sign as an intensification of a distinctively Christian view of language and meaning, and the thrust of his thinking is towards 'creating' history modelled upon a Trinitarian and incarnational understanding of participation. That is to return the divine gift, freely and imaginatively, and in a way, as Milbank would argue, that creates vital and new cultural possibilities of Christian life. This is a highly original and gladly provocative way of combining a radically deconstructive view of language with a meaningful philosophy of the self and a dynamically Christian theology of culture. But the philosophical positions embedded within it must be interrogated in the light of Christian faith. These are finally not *de fide*, for all the learned rhetoric of *Theology and Social Theory* and *The Word Made Strange* which might urge us to think otherwise. Rather, by reading Christianity through the lens of 'radical incommensurability' and 'writing', Milbank has closed out the speech agent, and therefore the sociality of language, which is predicated upon the innately dialogical character of utterance. His philosophical obligations serve therefore to construct an essentially *monological* and *heroic* view of culture.

While this affirms the centrality of language and culture to human identity and action, in a very welcome way, it also understands culture to be a task to which the exceptionally 'poetical' or gifted Christian individual is summoned in the interests of creating Christianity anew as transfiguration and theophany. Deconstructed language, no longer tied to reality or to other speakers, becomes the vehicle for a heroic re-sacralisation of the world carried out on behalf of the community by a solitary individual who possesses exceptional powers of divine poeticity. Both 'radical incommensurability' and 'writing' support creative, monological readings of history which are unhampered by the common space of dialogue with others. Nowhere is this more clear than in Milbank's abbreviated and naïve use of the term narrative. Where can a narrative be said to begin and end? Are we to take it that Christianity constitutes a single narrative? Or does it not in fact represent a complex interplay of narratives: Catholic and Protestant, Greek and Latin, Mediæval and modern, conservative and liberal? It would certainly seem to be the case that the history of the Church shows the internal collision of Christian narratives, across linguistic, cultural, historical and doctrinal divides. The *de facto* assumption that there is a single Christian narrative again bypasses areas of difficulty, and supports the single voice as solitary herald of unified Christian tradition.

Furthermore, the narrative which John Milbank seeks persuasively to perform is a distinctively Christian semiosis of non-violence. And yet the very notion of 'writing' itself contains violence: violence towards the one who speaks and to those with whom they speak. Pragmatic theorists rightly draw our attention to the fact that language finds its originary site in the dialogue between speakers which is specific to time and place. This is the sociality of language, in which speakers interact open-endedly with each other, in the actual construction of social relations. Cultural texts of course play a part here, which the speakers differentially inhabit, and the process of what Michael Silverstein has called "entextualisation" (whereby linguistic blocks are sedimented from fluid cultural processes as 'texts') is a vital way of creating cross-generational points of linguistic orientation: foci of shared norms and values.[25] But text as such (in the sense of Levinas' 'said') is itself the product of speech as encounter (Levinas' 'saying'), where the textualities of culture that are vehicles of meaning and identity are woven from within a mutuality of speech. This is an elusive moment of personal presence, in which the other both remains within the boundaries of the known and transcends them, supporting and sustaining a presence to self which likewise rests in self-possession and self-transcendence.

This is a sphere of *possibility* then, in which we can become something more than we have been: summoned to a higher or better existence by the presence of the other to ourselves in the interaction and encounter which is speech. For the Christian community it is precisely this excessive sphere of personal presence which becomes the site of revelation. This is the case firstly in so far as the presence of those in need can become the presence to us of Jesus himself. Selfishness is to ignore or to occlude the voices of the marginalised, while the Christian ethic springs from the belief that Jesus speaks to us through them.[26] But, secondly, our opening out to the presence of the personal other, which is given by the dialogism of language, is fulfilled in the unique presence to us of Jesus Christ in the Eucharist. It is here that we

25  Silverstein, M., and Urban, G., eds., *Natural Histories of Discourse*, Chicago, University of Chicago Press, 1996, pp. 1-17.
26  Matthew 25 [35-40].

recognise him once again as one who is with us, offered in encounter and engagement with our own reality, standing creatively at the heart of our cultural and social existence.

As Paul Ricœur has observed, it is a characteristic of religion not just to mark the transition of speech into text, but also, remarkably, to effect the conversion of written language back into oral communication.[27] Within the linguistic boundaries of the liturgy, scriptural texts become voices, the people speak with God, and God, in the real presence, once more speaks with his people. Human existence in all its complexity entails a pulsation therefore between sedimented textualities, passed from generation to generation in which sacred narrativities of new identity and existence are inscribed, and the saying that is speech, in which self and other coexist in a mutuality of the present, in the opening journey of reciprocal listening.

The relation of theologians with philosophers must always be one of listening and of dialogue, but it is an interaction which – for theologians – is under the sign of the unsurpassable dialogue of God with his people. Philosophical speech then has to be measured and weighed against the ways in which God has spoken with us, in the revelations which faith proclaims. John Milbank has done an enormous service for us by articulating a faith that is so much at ease with deconstructive philosophy and by using that philosophy so creatively for the purposes of a Christian 'metasemiosis'. But without the dialogism that is speech, we shall wonder where the interlocutors are, with whom we are formed into the body of the Church, and where the voice of God is, who is still sacramentally present with us today, and who poses to us, as to previous generations, the disturbing question: "But who do you say that I am?".[28]

27  Ricœur, P., *Figuring the Sacred*, translated by Pellauer, D., Minneapolis, Augsburg Press, 1995, p. 71.
28  Matthew 16 [15].

Chapter Nine

# Listening at the Threshold
# Christology and the
# "Suspension of the Material"

Lucy Gardner

## Introduction

*Not all noise is music; nor all music noise*

A simple observation, which serves to introduce the heart of the more complex problematic[1] this essay aims to suggest and the approach to Radical Orthodoxy[2] it traces: 'Listening at the threshold' to this collection of disparate voices, what sense do I, or can any of us, make of what we hear?

It would be trivial to make anything of the point that the authors of Radical Orthodoxy do not all 'sing the same tune' or say the same thing; clearly they do not. As Catherine Pickstock's sustained reflection upon Augustine's melodious metaphysics suggests, unison and homophony are not the only (and perhaps not the best) forms of music. The question seems to be rather, does

---

1  Further consideration of the genre of 'problematics' would no doubt yield much of theological significance, not least in the light of Radical Orthodoxy's assessment of *aporia,* which appears on occasion as that which is to be resolved and surpassed (e.g. *Radical Orthodoxy*, p. 37, note 49), but on others as that which is properly irresolvable (e.g. *Radical Orthodoxy*, pp. 113; 269).

2  The term is used to apply to both the book of that title and the 'movement' associated with it, whilst it is recognised: first, that the public identity of that 'movement' is somewhat obscure; second, that not all the authors in the volume subscribe to all the views here considered; and third, not everything that any of the authors has written is to be considered as part of the movement.

this polyphony, for all its dissonance, resolve into any contrapuntal harmony? If so, when? And where do I have to stand in order to hear this noise as music? Indeed, where do I have to be in order to hear any echo of the Divine?[3]

The problem is one of proportion and, as it were, perspective (a cross invocation which already directs attention to the 'convolutions' of the senses in our 'perceiving' anything at all, a theme to which the second section of this essay turns). Reflecting on the essays of *Radical Orthodoxy*, I find myself trying to articulate a problem of my relation to that which I would understand; a problem which has to do with the nature of meaning and the theological desire for appropriate speech.

Put bluntly, the problem is this: at the heart of Radical Orthodoxy I find a call for non-oppositional opposition, or, more properly speaking, an undoing of opposition in a non-oppositional way.[4] This is a position which will find itself 'grounded' (if we can think such a thought today) in the Eucharist, the Church, Christ and ultimately the Trinitarian life. This is not least because, for Radical Orthodoxy, this is the only possible authentic grounding for anything and everything, including Being itself.

This stance is clearly commensurate with catholic theology. At the same time, however, Radical Orthodoxy exhibits the rhetoric and the exercise of a very powerful *oppositional* opposition, which talks of this undoing not only, as one would expect, in terms of a refusal[5] of the oppositions of secularised discourse (including most modern theology), but also in terms of an

---

3  Perhaps we must say at least this: for all its contingency, music, which may indeed be "the science which most leads towards theology" (*Radical Orthodoxy*, p. 243), is never 'accidental'; it requires at least the minimal 'intentionality' of a listener, if not of an orchestrator – and although possibly minimal, this intentionality is a complex and demanding labour; itself an exercise in harmony.

4  The call assumes many different guises, and deploys several sets of vocabulary. This phrasing (the non-oppositional undoing of opposition) is suggested by a note to Michael Hanby's essay on desire (*Radical Orthodoxy*, p. 125, note 53). See below for full citation and further elaboration.

5  Radical Orthodoxy *does* speak in these terms; see, e.g., *Radical Orthodoxy*, p. 2 (Radical Orthodoxy "[refuses] all 'mediations' through other spheres of knowledge and culture"); *Radical Orthodoxy*, p. 3 (Radicalism "refuses the secular"); *Radical Orthodoxy*, p. 111 (Augustine's thought is to be reclaimed as "decidedly anti-metaphysical [in the secular sense] for its refusal to fix these borders").

effacement and a blurring[6] of those oppositions. Creation itself, and not only redemption, is presented as a perpetual "crossing-out" of substantiality.[7] This prompts me to ask: What is the status and the significance of the seeming violence of this imagery? To what extent does it participate in the "politics of noise"[8] – the violence of shouting down and silencing others – which Radical Orthodoxy would shun? Is it a necessary part of the "suspension of the material"[9] to which Radical Orthodoxy would witness, or is it an elision of that suspension?

It seems immediately necessary to indicate that this is not simply a problem or a question concerning the elegance and success or otherwise of rhetoric. The difficulty here is not just that a certain rhetoric of the non-oppositional undoing of opposition turns out to be wearily and inevitably self-defeating. There are acutely theological and specifically Christological issues at stake here. The phrasing of this conundrum (the non-oppositional undoing of opposition) comes not from any self-description of Radical Orthodoxy, but from a discussion of Augustine's theory of atonement in a note to Michael Hanby's essay on desire. It describes the work of atonement – the work of the Word of God. Drawing on reflections from Graham Ward's reflections on the displaced body of Christ in his contribution to the volume, Hanby suggests that:

> Only this displacement, combined with Jesus' volitional obedience, i.e. his *doxological* exchange with the Father, can avoid making death and the cross, rather than Jesus' continence and innocence, the meaningful moment in God.

6   The language and the difficulty is perhaps most apparent in William Cavanaugh's essay which must attempt to tell the difficult and strained relationship of the Church to the oppositions of the secular world: "in the Eucharist the foundational distinction between mine and thine is radically effaced (cf. Acts 2 [44-47])". (*Radical Orthodoxy*, p. 195); and, "this eschatological gathering is neither an entirely worldly nor an entirely other-worldly event, but blurs the lines between the temporal and the eternal" (*Radical Orthodoxy*, p. 185).

7   *Radical Orthodoxy*, p. 248.

8   *Radical Orthodoxy*, p. 19.

9   The phrase constitutes the intriguing subtitle to *Radical Orthodoxy*, and yet is alluded to only once (to my recollection) – in an account of its provocation within the work of Jacobi and Hamann in the Introduction (*Radical Orthodoxy*, p. 3): 'suspension' does not occur in the index, whilst the 'material' must be sought under 'materiality' and is discussed in only one essay.

Together they allow one to think an atonement theory wherein Jesus can both undercut and redeem that opposition, refuse salvific efficacy to the violence itself, and leave the hope, relative to justice for instance, that the resurrection does not simply 'transcend' evil, but reverses and 'undoes' it.[10]

The questions this raises are Christological. They have primarily to do with relationships to Christ, which are complicated by the fact that these relationships (even that of 'opposition') depend on a participation in Christ. They are, then, questions to do with how we are to think and speak about that Word in which we already participate, but in which we are called to participate more fully.[11] What relations does (should) the work wrought by the words of theology bear to the work of this Word?

These questions therefore also have to do with the nature of 'meaning', and in particular its relationship to materiality. How is such an atonement theory to be thought without 'undoing' the materiality of Christ's displacement and obedience, of the cross and his death, and of the violence and evil which attend them? How are we to think such a theory of atonement without, as it were, replacing (displacing) materiality with meaning and volition, and thus undoing the materiality of words and thought themselves? To what extent does a translation into thought 'undo', or at least stall, theories of atonement?

In preparation for an expansion of these questions, let me suggest two distinct aspects to this problem. The first aspect concerns the problem of the determination of place or the language of relation. Listening at the threshold, I find myself neither 'in' nor 'out' of Radical Orthodoxy, unable to find any clear relation to it. At one level this is a question of the historical accidents of biography. I have neither studied nor worked in Cambridge, and this time two years ago I was proudly nursing my six-week-old son.

Yet, this unforgivably autobiographical introduction[12] provokes the burden of this paper, which emerges as a question concerning the 'proper'

---

10 *Radical Orthodoxy*, p. 125, note 53. See below, II, a, *The Displacement of Christology*, for a more detailed consideration of this theme.
11 Compare Colossians 2[10].
12 The phrase is suggested by Jean-Luc Marion's startling yet familiar insight that "one must obtain forgiveness for every essay in theology". *God Without Being*, translated by Carlson, T. A., Chicago, Chicago University Press, 1991, p. 2 (*Dieu sans l'être*, Paris, Librairie Arthème Fayard, 1981, p. 10).

(Christological) displacement of Christology; for at another, no doubt more 'significant'[13] level, this question about the language of relation has to do with *anyone's* difficulty in finding a relation to the thought of Radical Orthodoxy. This is because one of the movement's central and explicit themes is the problematisation of space and relation (and in particular the notions of 'in' and 'out') in the first place, on account of the pursuit of a lost sense of participation.[14] But this apparently leads to an intriguing double-think: everything is 'in' – within theology, within Radical Orthodoxy, within Christology – except strong and thick demarcations of inside and outside.

This theme is clearly evidenced in Catherine Pickstock's work, which highlights modernity's spatialisation of time. It is also to be found in John Milbank's and Michael Hanby's appropriations of Augustine. The attraction of this problematisation seems in part to be the fundamentally pragmatic presumption that strong demarcations of 'in' and 'out' are not only undesirable as such (on aesthetic and logical grounds at least, if not ethical), but that they are in fact unserviceable. Since they are always either too rigid for the representation of reality's plasticity, or too plastic and unstable to support any representation, they will always fail. Indeed, it is this recognition which suggests a need for reflection upon "the suspension of the material". The question is whether such a strong position on the inadequacies of the rhetoric of 'in' and 'out' as that taken by Radical Orthodoxy, with insufficient attention to its own necessary subsequent deployment of this same conceptuality, will be able to sustain such a reflection.

---

13  It has, that is, to do more obviously with the event of meaning than with the meaning of events.

14  The phrase "lost sense of participation" serves repeatedly to diagnose the malady of modernity. See, e.g., *Radical Orthodoxy*, p. 7; p. 14. The difficulty here to be considered is how such a sense of participation is to be retrieved once it has been (all but) lost. There is a sense in which only participation can grant a sense of participation: we cannot simply generate this sense for ourselves; and yet, as Radical Orthodoxy writers recognise, the ancient world in which this sense of participation was so all-pervasive that it was barely visible and nevertheless always sensed is now virtually closed to us. Today, our sense of participation arrives precisely as our sense of its (that is our) loss.

The second aspect of my problem concerns difficulties of language about language, or the relation of language.[15] Again, this problem is clearly a central and explicit theme of Radical Orthodoxy.[16] Of greater interest is the fact that it has a direct bearing upon the specifically Christological consideration of words about the Word, precisely in the impropriety of any attempt to establish the logic of talking about Christ apart from talking about him.

Some indication of this Christological direction of my thought might be given with reference to a provocative question to be found in the central pages of *Radical Orthodoxy*. Reflecting upon the "broken line" of Anselm's *Proslogion*[17] and Balthasar's suggestion that the founding of the joy of aesthetic reason on the suffering of the Son of God "casts a long shadow over the whole theological aesthetic", David Moss asks, in perceptive recognition of the catastrophe at stake here, the following question:

> What sort of shadow? A reversal that would explode every perceptible proportion in the existential structures of mortal life, friendship included?[18]

To my mind, the debates over Radical Orthodoxy's theological location obscure a more fundamental question concerning Christology and the atonement. What happens to our view of the world when we learn to see it as

15 My opening observation could be translated and inverted in a somewhat more obviously Heideggerian idiom, thus: Not all words (language) are poetry; nor is poetry all words. The initial observation and to some extent my title were, in part, prompted by Christopher Fynsk's book *Noise at the Threshold: Language and Relation, That There is Language,* Stanford, Stanford University Press, 1996, pp. 17-38. Fynsk undertakes a suggestive reading of Heidegger's comments (in his 1953 essay *Georg Trakl. Eine Erörterung seines Gedichts*: reprinted in *Unterwegs zur Sprache*, Pfullingen, Neske, 1959 [*On the Way to Language*, New York, Harper & Row, 1971]) on George Trakl's poem "A Winter's Evening". They were also provoked by Catherine Pickstock's intricate and determinative reflections upon the "metaphysics" of Augustine's *de Musica*.

16 The primary essay here is clearly Conor Cunningham's on Language (*Radical Orthodoxy*, pp. 64-90). My argument is not simply an accusation of blindness to the problems of the spatialising aspects of conceptuality, nor to the problems of conceptuality (language) itself. My suggestion is rather that there seems to be in Radical Orthodoxy a structural blindness and deafness to its own failures to follow through the theological implications of its treatment of these issues in a systematic and consequential manner.

17 The phrase is Henri de Lubac's.

18 *Radical Orthodoxy*, p. 139.

grounded in a non-grounding way in the Lamb slain from the beginning of the world? What sort of meaning can we see in this death and this making? What sort of a world does this non-grounding 'make'? What sort of reason can begin to be grasped by it? And how are we to move from other mis-understandings to this understanding, and the fullness of its consequences?

My task here, as I attend to the dissonances and resonances of my reading of Radical Orthodoxy – as I try to listen to what Radical Orthodoxy *says* and *how* it says it in its well-ordered and highly wrought compositions – is to pursue some of the trajectories suggested by my autobiographical difficulty (concerning the intellectual, ethical and political torsions of human identity and 'relating') and thus to sketch a series of questions for further reflection. I focus on the two aspects of my problem (the language of relation and the relation of language) in turn. I view each aspect from two different angles. These reflections yield a Christological configuration for the binding of these two aspects in each other.

To anticipate in summary: the hesitations I feel about Radical Orthodoxy's programme for the recovery of a lost sense of participation combine an uneasiness at the powerful Christology which lies at its heart and frames it with a disquiet at the relatively simplistic (albeit technically sophisticated) problematisations of perception, spatiality and sense, with a disturbed sense of surprise at the apparent lack of awareness of (if not, contrariwise, on occasion, a positive delight in) the catastrophic explosions/implosions which have been set in train. In short, I find the experience of 'listening at the threshold' an experience determined by equal measures of profound gratitude and growing alarm.

## First Aspect – The Language of Relation and Location

The difficulties of the relations of participation, of discerning 'insides' and 'outsides', and conceiving appropriate 'thresholds' and 'middles', are themselves evidenced in potential difficulties concerning Radical Orthodoxy's own location. These, in their turn, provoke the difficulty of finding a relation to the movement. I therefore discuss this aspect with reference, first, to

Radical Orthodoxy's *theological* location and second, to its *historical* positioning.

## Theological Location

Behind the robust intellectual engagement with the "sites in which secularism has invested heavily"[19] lies Radical Orthodoxy's demand that all *scientia* be granted – and recognise – its proper theological place. For this reason at least it may prove fruitful to reflect upon Radical Orthodoxy's location (and thus the location of my problematic) not so much within the history of theology as with reference to the 'framework'[20] of Christian Theology itself.

From a somewhat Barthian viewpoint, the broadly apologetic intent of the Radical Orthodoxy project must be situated somewhere within the question of the anti-relation between natural theology and Prolegomena: it is too theological and confessional to be 'philosophy' or mere 'critical theory'; but it is too concerned with metaphysics and secular themes to be 'genuine' theology. This Barthian unplaceablity, together with the recognisably apologetic-polemic rhythm of Radical Orthodoxy's endeavours, however, suggests a rather different identification as an exercise in something like Schleiermacher's 'Philosophical Theology'.[21] Certainly, it is only from some

---

19 *Radical Orthodoxy*, p. 1.

20 I return to consider Radical Orthodoxy's own relationship to this metaphor of a 'framework' of Christian Theology under my second aspect.

21 As well as providing a site from which such a conversation *might* be conducted at the same time as colonising philosophy, without betraying the theology of inclusion espoused, this identification also helps explain the paradigmatic nature of Radical Orthodoxy's apparently unavoidable "conversation" with "philosophy" and "metaphysics". But this only serves to name, rather than resolve, any difficulty concerning Radical Orthodoxy's relationship to philosophy and metaphysics. For, in Radical Orthodoxy (as to some extent in Schleiermacher's theology), theology, Christians and theologians alike must cast a negative judgement upon modernity's fiction of an autonomous reason (on account of its presumption of a Godless stance, and its aporetic and nihilistic conclusions); in thus "evaluating philosophy" and "surpassing the aporetic", they will in fact "*save* reason [from itself, for God] and fulfil and preserve philosophy, whereas philosophy left to itself, brings itself, as Heidegger saw, to its own end" (*Radical Orthodoxy*, p. 37). Reason is not merely to be denied or dismissed out of hand; it should have a place in theology. At the same time, there should be no place for autonomous, nihilistic reason within theology. The task of rediscovering or reclaiming a lost sense of participation does not merely mean convincing

such theological position that Radical Orthodoxy can be 'theology', whilst 'conversing' with "philosophy" and "secularism" *and* "visiting" traditional theological sites, without contradicting itself.

There are of course many such doctrinal "sites" which Radical Orthodoxy "visits" and develops. The most clearly articulated is perhaps that of a sustained reflection upon the implications of a faithful and thorough-going account of the creation *ex nihilo*.[22] Another location whose plasticity is less obviously tested and stretched by Radical Orthodoxy is that of ecclesiology.[23] These, however, both seem in turn, within systematic theology and Radical Orthodoxy alike, to find their place within the broader narrative of sanctification.[24]

One reading of Radical Orthodoxy is that it accepts the challenge of the important and difficult task of telling this narrative. Indeed, there is a sense in which Radical Orthodoxy's pursuit of our lost sense of participation represents a bold[25] and confident attempt to project a programme for transfiguration or construct a politics of transformation. But here, *both* in terms of Radical Orthodoxy's insistence on a theology of inclusion *and* in terms of the redemption and sanctification of that which already only has its

     reason that it does in fact participate in the mind of God (inviting it, as it were, 'back' into theology, when it never really left) but also requires the expulsion of false reason from theology; another instance of the apparently violent forms which the (non-oppositional) undoing of opposition will assume.

22 This interest is itself, of course, an indicator of historical location, in that the determining conversation partner for Radical Orthodoxy is the 'nihilism' which has so marked the twentieth century.

23 This was perhaps first 'noticed' by Gillian Rose in her lively appreciation of John Milbank's *Theology and Society* and her fierce critique of its "ecclesiology of mending". (See Rose, G., *The Broken Middle*, Oxford, Basil Blackwell, 1992, pp. 277-296.) There is a sense in which this paper can only hope to open these reflections from a different angle, for the Christological difficulties it explores will require ecclesiological inflection if they are to be properly understood. Christian theology will always be the words and work of the Church, and will always take the *form* of a particular relationship to Christ.

24 The subtitle to this paper in its conference form referred to "Spatial Metaphor in Narratives of Sanctification", an allusion to the title of the session in which it occurred (Sanctifying the Profane) which intended to indicate this particular convolution of the conceptuality of Christian Theology.

25 Indeed "unprecedented boldness" is presented as a description of the movement's critical approach and stance, and is claimed as one of the intended senses of the designation "Radical". (*Radical Orthodoxy*, p. 2)

being in God, the difficulty of recovering a lost sense of participation can be seen as that of how to 'bring in' that which is in some sense always already in.[26]

The difficulties of 'locating' Radical Orthodoxy, and thus also the difficulties of its paradigmatic relation to philosophy, in terms of which I am attempting to demonstrate the difficulty of language of relation, receive a new inflection in consideration of the construal of Radical Orthodoxy's historical positioning.

## (Anti-)Historical Positioning: Opposing Opposition

As I have already suggested, fundamental to the Radical Orthodoxy programme, and to its own sense of identity, is a story of opposition: opposition to modernity's secularism and its so-called "nihilism". In constructing itself as *for* an "orthodox" and "radical" "commitment to credal Christianity and the exemplarity of its patristic matrix",[27] Radical Orthodoxy *first* presents itself as *against* modernity and much of postmodernity.

The history which Radical Orthodoxy must narrate in order to articulate its own identity involves a genealogy of error, an archaeology of sorts – an

---

26 The difficulties I am attempting to articulate are not necessarily peculiar to Radical Orthodoxy. In so far as they are difficulties of language, they are difficulties which appear whenever and wherever anyone tries to reflect upon or speak about language. In so far as they are difficulties of telling the process of change, whilst working within or for that process, they are very general, perhaps even universal, human difficulties. And, of course, in so far as they are difficulties of proclaiming the Gospel and working for the Kingdom of God, they are theological difficulties to be faced by any Christian theologian at least, if not any Christian. And in that they are also difficulties concerning the question as to how to bring in those who are already in, they are indicative of the peculiar problem of ecclesial existence 'in the world but not of it'. Nevertheless, they are another inflection of the difficulties of a rediscovery of our lost sense of participation: how are we to come to participate in this sense again? We have not ceased to participate in the world, nor in God; we are simply no longer capable of sensing these facts. It is as if our spiritual senses have been dulled in the attempts to iron out their convolutions; is the attempt to re-sensitise them as futile as the attempt to restore its saltiness to salt which has lost its flavour?

27 *Radical Orthodoxy*, p. 2.

answer to the question: what went wrong, where?[28] For Radical Orthodoxy, what went wrong in the late Middle Ages, and thus at, and as, the cleaving of modernity (a cleaving of itself from its past and a cleaving to itself, to its own presence and the bad infinite of its quasi-eternal 'now'), was the false division of philosophy from theology (of reason, knowledge or science from faith and revelation). Reason sought to slip the leash of faith, whilst theology thought it expedient to allow it to do so, in a pale imitation of, and a distorted participation in, its new interpretation of the freedom and divine prescience of the God who allowed creation the freedom to follow its own mind and will. It is this which is described as the "loss of a sense of participation"[29] in the Divine life.

The task to be firmly grasped by Radical Orthodoxy, then, is quite clearly the (non-oppositional) undoing of these oppositions (a reversal and a recapitulation of these reversals) and a rediscovery of that lost sense of participation.[30] This is a difficult task, made the more so by the fact that these

28 In this itself we might recognise Radical Orthodoxy's ambiguous relationship to both modernity and postmodernity as not that of simple opposition. To tell a beginning at all, of course, and the beginning of modernity in particular, is a peculiarly modern undertaking. One might suggest that modernity is nothing other than the perpetual re-fabrication of its own lost beginnings, its account of itself as the 'new time', the now, the present. The difference here, of course, (a difference which will often earn the title *post*-modern) is that these beginnings are told against modernity. And in finding a different account of these beginnings, Radical Orthodoxy, along with other contemporary commentators and critics (to name three largely arbitrary examples: Lyotard, J.-F., *Leçons sur l'analytique du sublime*, Paris, Editions Galilée, 1991, translated by Rottenberg, E., as *Lessons on the Analytic of the Sublime*, Stanford, Stanford University Press, 1994; Deleuze, G., *Le Pli: Leibniz et le Baroque*, Paris, Les Editions de Minuit, translated by Conley, T., as *The Fold: Leibniz and the Baroque*, London, Athlone Press, 1993; Dupré, L., *Passage to Modernity – an Essay in the Hermeneutics of Nature and Culture*, London, Yale University Press, 1996), exposes misunderstandings of modernity, not least those inscribed, as it were, at its very heart - its own self-(mis)understanding, one might (almost) say.

29 Cf. *Radical Orthodoxy*, pp.7; 14.

30 The fundamental insight is not new; in its basic outline it is to be found, for example, in the opening pages of Hans Urs von Balthasar's *Herrlichkeit* trilogy – an affinity (if not direct influence) witnessed to by the careful and extensive *Auseinandersetzung* with Balthasar's diagnosis and attempted remedy in the *Introduction* to *Radical Orthodoxy*. (Von Balthasar, H. U., *Herrlichkeit: Eine Theologische Ästhetik*, Einsiedeln, Johannes Verlag, 1961, Vol. 1, *Schau der Gestalt* [translated by Leiva-Merikakis, E. as *The Glory of the Lord*, Edinburgh, T & T Clark, 1982, Vol. 1, *Seeing the Form*]; see also *Radical Orthodoxy*, pp.12-

divisions have been inverted in the secularised world – it is not simply that reason has separated from faith, but that reason now regards faith as a departure from reason.

At this point, Radical Orthodoxy appears to be in an unseemly haste to embrace the opportunities offered by (post-) modernity, in the guise of "sites" to be re-visited, re-situated and re-worked, and to pass rather too easily over the historical reality of these reversals and oppositions, and the marks that they have made on the world and in human reason.[31] It is almost as if realising what is necessary (seeing or understanding the need for the recovery of a lost sense of participation) will suffice to replace the labour of the recovery for which this recognition calls. What is the difference between such a position and an espousal of the voluntarist 'theology of will' with which Radical Orthodox suggests modern politics has replaced the patristic and Mediæval "theology of participation"?[32] And what are we to make of this position's apparent obliviousness to the power and the violence – to the politics – which it inveighs?

The point here is not merely the near customary observation of deconstruction that implicit structure works against explicit intention. For, in this, Radical Orthodoxy seems strangely anti-historical. The reality of these divisions (and thus of this history) is called into question by the metaphors of violent removal to which I have already alluded. If there is no violence here, then has the invalidity of that which this language opposes been made unreal within the world of Radical Orthodoxy? If, on the other hand, these divisions *are* real, and are to be effaced, then what does this effacement have to do with either the "suspension of the material" and its interruptions, or the pacific introduction of peace (the undoing of oppositional opposition)?

18 in particular.) Of particular interest here is the accusation that, at times, Balthasar remains disappointingly modern. A similar point can be made about Radical Orthodoxy's approach to "history", which insists that we do not read modernity's "sites" back into earlier writers (the modern self into Augustine's *Confessions*, for example), whilst itself apparently reading every ancient error in terms of and as a precursor to modernity's predicament, its divisions and its nihilism.

31 For all its groundlessness and self-doubt, for all its "illusory" character, the modern subject, for example, exists. It is there – even illusions have a reality. Radical Orthodoxy's tendency to ignore these implications threatens the texture of the carefully constructed inter-textuality of ideality and reality for which it also argues.

32 See, for example, Cavanaugh's citation of Milbank, *Radical Orthodoxy*, p. 186.

There are quite clearly theological implications at stake here. Moreover, Radical Orthodoxy's central opposition is to what it terms "nihilism". This determination is reflected no doubt in Radical Orthodoxy's recovery of a doctrine of creation *ex nihilo*. Put crudely, Radical Orthodoxy seeks to articulate the place that (the) nothing takes in the order of things, rather than allowing it to play a role as the 'ground' (or 'non-ground') of everything – the indeterminacy ('chaos') from which determinacy ('order') miraculously and aporetically emerges, and to which it appears destined to return. The question here, however, is whether the refusal of a reduction to indeterminacy will approximate to a "hovering close" to nihilism,[33] or whether it will in fact implicate Radical Orthodoxy far more radically in the "nothingness" of the "denial" which it thus sets out to refuse.[34]  Closer attention to the term 'nihilism', and indeed to Radical Orthodoxy's construction of its opponent, are called for here, but must remain largely beyond the scope of this paper.[35] Nevertheless, mention of this relation serves as a more provocative example of the difficulties of (op)position for a theology of participation and of the ambiguity of Radical Orthodoxy's own historical and theological location, than that of the more general difficulties of theology's (and Radical Orthodoxy's) relation to philosophy.  It also introduces a theme which begs a Christological attention.

---

33  *Radical Orthodoxy*, p. 1.

34  Cf. *Radical Orthodoxy*, p. 247.

35  Radical Orthodoxy constructs itself as the only viable rational alternative to nihilism (see *Radical Orthodoxy*, p. 4), and understands nihilism as that to which all other thought (including secularised theology) can be reduced, as the inevitable trajectory of secularism's denial of God.  See Laurence Hemming's contribution to the same volume, *Nihilism: Heidegger and the Grounds of Redemption* (*Radical Orthodoxy*, pp. 91-108), for the more radical and contradictory suggestion of the need (and the possibility) to turn *through* (Heidegger's) "nihilism" (not to be construed as the pathological desire for nothing) rather than simply veering from it, as seems rather to be the case within the main architecture of Radical Orthodoxy.

## Second Aspect – The Relation of Language and the Convolutions of Sense[36]

Under this aspect, I discuss the question of the nature of language itself: first in terms of a consideration of a Christological oddity in *Radical Orthodoxy* – evidenced in both the *Introduction* and Graham Ward's essay *Bodies: The Displaced Body of Christ*;[37] and second with reference to the ambiguities of the use of the predominantly spatial metaphor "theological framework".

### *The Displacement of Christology*

In the concise opening paragraphs of the Introduction, it is claimed that Radical Orthodoxy attempts "to reclaim the world by situating its concerns and activities within a theological framework".[38] This is to be achieved by "resituating" modernity's thematic "sites" "from a Christian standpoint; that is, in terms of the Trinity, Christology, the Church and the Eucharist".[39] The list of theological terms surely refers to central and connected themes, which together serve to denote "Christian Theology", but there is a telling oddity here, which might almost be missed: placed alongside Trinity, the Church and Eucharist, we find, not Christ, but Christology.

In the light of Graham Ward's essay on the thoroughly Johannine theme of the properly Christological displacement of Christ's Body, and thus always of Christ, this oddity should not be dismissed as insignificant. Here, Christ, the Word of God, is displaced by words about Christ. Moreover, this oddity itself echoes the singularly odd omission of the scene of the Deposition (surely the paradigmatic moment in which Christ's Body, in all its materiality, is

---

36  The phrase "convolutions of sense" is suggested by the title to Moss' attentive reading of St Anselm's theological construal of friendship. It is here intended to describe the difficult, aporetic and elusive 'exchange', which is neither exclusively internal nor entirely external to any or all of us, in which meaning is made and found; that is to say, the ways in which sense (our reason and our senses) makes sense of the world, precisely in catching itself making sense in its (and our) interactions with the world, in the world. Greater attention to this 'logic' of exchange, I suggest, may well deepen our understanding of the logic of participation and our sense of it which are at issue here.
37  *Radical Orthodoxy*, pp. 163-181.
38  *Radical Orthodoxy*, p. 1.
39  *Radical Orthodoxy*, p. 1.

moved and displaced from one place to another, rather than simply banished from place altogether) from that essay's series of *tableaux* in which the displacement of Christ's Body is explored as a paradigm of the instability of created reality. Properly speaking, then, such an instability is not simply the instability between things and ideas (the material's perpetual evasion of capture by thought, our wearisome inaccessibility to ourselves), but rather the proper instability, the material displacement, of things as things, their very materiality, we might say.[40]

What seems to be lacking here is an attention to the attentive removal of the body, an 'abiding' with it and its mute materiality, as it moves from one suspension (the Cross) to another (Holy Saturday), suspended, as it were, not over-against the void but between suspensions. Attention to this attentive removal, which already consists in the interaction (the convolution) of the senses of sensory perception ('seeing' a 'mute' body), would in its turn demand reflection upon the 'intellectual' or 'spiritual' event of attending to this attention, an attention to the interactions between our sensory and our spiritual senses. It would require us to think a deposition 'in' thought, in which the cadaver (pure body, sheer material, in all its specific, finite, determinate, meaningless indeterminacy) is deposed 'into' thought, covered with thought and drenched with meaning, in a (retrospective) participatory anticipation of (and anticipatory participation in) the resurrection of that Body and its re-drenching with the Holy Spirit on Easter morning.

The omission from Ward's essay of this moment of the Gospel story, and with it the omission of an account of the movement, that is displacement, of the body, from body to thought, in thought, is paralleled by (participates in, intensifies and is intensified by) the volume's tendency to elide Christ with Christology, so that Christ is more obscured, eclipsed even, than witnessed to in a Christology which is itself thereby displaced from its proper displacement. This elision closes the (hermeneutical-political) gap between

---

40 This is a recognition which in its turn suggests that 'materiality' is not something (an 'idea') which thought bestows upon things (matter), but is precisely the manner in which matter gives itself to thought – whilst neither in fact giving itself over into thought, nor delivering an illusory and unsatisfactory 'copy' of itself. That which this exchange (the 'event' of meaning) most properly grants is precisely a trusting familiarity with and a participation in this exchange, the convolutions, of sense making sense.

language and that which language is about, and effects the 'coupling', or the confusion, of the two aspects of my problem within a Christological configuration/disfiguration of the second. There appears then to be a disturbance in the relation between the historical and the theological, between the material and the thoughtful – and this from within the volume's (the movement's?) Christology, in which one would expect to find Christian theological language rooted.[41] How are we to distinguish proper from improper Christological displacement?

## *Reclaiming the World – or (Re-)claiming a Theological Framework?*

The difficulty I am labouring to outline here can also be found in a three-fold ambiguity of the programmatic summary I have already quoted: Radical Orthodoxy claims to attempt "to reclaim the world by situating its concerns and activities within a theological framework".[42] This is to be achieved by "resituating" modernity's thematic "sites" "from a Christian standpoint".[43]

First, there is an ambiguity in what I have called the "language of relation": what exactly is 'in' the theological frame? There seem to be two possible referents: the act of situating and resituating, on the one hand; and the new sites thus granted on the other. Since these are not mutually exclusive, it is possible that both are in fact to be sited within the theological frame. This would seem to be the most likely reading, but the conclusion is cast in doubt

---

41 Does Christ's Body, in fact, as it were "anchor" thought (and analogy) by being "suspended" outside of thought? (Here a similarity may be noted to the logic which anchors analogy in women's bodies outlined in *Something like Time: Something like the Sexes*, Gardner, L. and Moss, D., in *Balthasar at the End of Modernity*.) To provide a more obviously material elaboration: Does the Sacred Heart of Jesus cease to exist (for us) as flesh and blood, and become merely an insightful theological circumlocution and a devotion to be either "loved" or despised?

42 *Radical Orthodoxy*, p. 1.

43 *Radical Orthodoxy*, p. 1. These "sites" represent, according to the *Introduction*, those "things" which secularity has apparently celebrated and yet in fact ruined and denied - embodied life, self-expression, sexuality, aesthetic experience, human political community. Radical Orthodoxy attempts a "rescue", to be effected by a transcendental "suspension" which at once "interrupts" these things and "upholds" "their relative worth over-against the void" (cf., in all cases, *Radical Orthodoxy*, p. 3). I shall have cause to return to the exact nature of this double suspension in my concluding section.

by the suggestion that the resituating is to be done *from* a Christian standpoint – looking out, as it were, onto other standpoints, which do not fall within the theological framework.

Second, and related to the first ambiguity, does the resituating thus envisaged constitute a 'bringing in'? If modernity's sites are to be resituated within a theological framework, does this mean that they are, in fact, not yet within that theological frame? If so, then this is problematic, since, as we have seen, Radical Orthodoxy does not recognise any 'outside' to theology – any such supposed 'outside' is invalid and illusory, non-existent even.[44] But if these sites are already within the frame, then what sort of 'resituation' is to be undertaken?

Is this nothing other than a volitional, voluntarist re-alignment of sight (and understanding), a clothing of the world in a different thinking, rather than any *de facto* resituation? This is in part not a problem in so far as the sites to be resituated are precisely sites for thought. And yet the spatial imagery seems to marshal more than was intended. We are left suspended, over-against the material (and so against Radical Orthodoxy's explicit will), within a certain realm of thought and ideality, unconnected with the material. This ambiguity thus touches upon both the language of relation *and* the relation of language, and shows that the first ambiguity also operates within the second aspect of my problematic.

The third ambiguity of this programmatic outline also combines both these aspects, and yet operates primarily within the second – the question of the relation of language (and particularly of language about language): what is the meaning of the word 'framework' here? Is theology a 'frame' – a border, a limit concept, the demarcation of a territory – of which things can be, hypothetically at least, 'in' or 'out'? The phrase "within a theological framework" would seem to imply that it is. Or is the framework of theology rather more like a skeleton, a structure, an articulation or a system of linkages, with a centre but no circumscribable edges, as other passages in the *Introduction* suggest?

---

44 See, e.g. John Milbank's explication (*Radical Orthodoxy*, p. 37) of the ground for his *rejection* of "social science" performed in his earlier book, *Theology and Social Theory: Beyond Secular Reason*, Oxford, Basil Blackwell, 1990, in contradistinction to the colonising of philosophy in *Radical Orthodoxy*.

These ambiguities are critical for Radical Orthodoxy's programme, for its "central theological framework is 'participation' as developed by Plato and reworked by Christianity, because any alternative configuration perforce reserves a territory independent of God".[45] But 'participation' (particularly when conceived in terms of harmony) is a difficult concept, which provokes *both* the relational difficulties of the conceptuality of 'in' and 'out' *and* the linguistic, rhetorical dissonances of language of removal (that which refuses participation must be ejected) – the two aspects of my problematic.

This series of ambiguities might therefore be translated into the question: What is the relation (the difference) between participation in theology and participation in God? This in turn could be inflected in a question concerning the relationships between human and divine reason – between God, God's words, the Word of God, and our words about God. Is there a double sense here in which, whilst there is no 'territory reserved independent of God', both 'reason' and 'participation' are somehow reserved *from* us, *for* God? This is a problematic which, for Christian theology at least, will require the mediation of Christological-ecclesiological deliberations.

## Conclusion – Suspending the Material?

In pursuing an autobiographical yet thoroughly theological difficulty, I have attempted to articulate a series of hesitations about the rhetoric deployed by Radical Orthodoxy in its attempt to reawaken a lost sense of participation and thereby reclaim the world, the city and the soul. An attention to the instabilities and limitations of spatial metaphor (the question of the language of relation) and to the nature of language itself (the question of the relation of language) has yielded two further sets of questions:

First, Ecclesiological-Christological questions of gathering. These may be described as follows: How is sanctification to come about? How are we to tell this event? How is all that is, which already only has its being in and 'through' the Word, to be 'brought into' Christ? And how are we to recover a proper sense of our proper participation?

Second, questions of properly theological language: How are we to speak

---

45 *Radical Orthodoxy*, p. 3.

in such a way as not to undo the inter-textuality of the ideal and the real in our speaking? How are we to portray rather than betray the proper relation, that is again the *participation* of words in the world, and of the world in the Word?

These two areas of questioning in turn, and in particular their coincidence with respect to Christology, have suggested a Christological disturbance. The disturbance is surely not unique to Radical Orthodoxy. Any Christian theology must be troubled by the relation between its own words and the Word. And more so by the events of the cross in which this relation is released. In Radical Orthodoxy, however, we are presented with quite particular and acutely contemporary configurations of these troubles, not least in the apparent failure to thematise them sufficiently.[46]

It is thus in recognition as much of a debt owed the authors of Radical Orthodoxy as of the provocations of their theology that I close with a brief, suggestive and preliminary gathering of my observations into a series of issues for further inquiry:

(i) What places are to be granted or recognised for the *nihil* and chaos in the Christology and the doctrines of sanctification and redemption from which the doctrine of creation *ex nihilo* emerges? (Here the question for Radical Orthodoxy is whether it hovers too close to nihilism – or not close enough.[47])

(ii) "Yet what finally distances [Radical Orthodoxy] from nihilism is its proposal of the rational possibility, and the faithfully perceived actuality, of an indeterminacy that is not impersonal chaos but infinite interpersonal harmonious order."[48] How are we to exercise that faithful judgement (which takes its measure from Christological proportion) of the differences between

46  It should, however, be noted that something of an antidote (and not therapy) is offered in the essays of Cavanaugh and Moss, in that these both offer richly textured and non-oppositional accounts of the labours of Christian relation and its forms of life.

47  Hemming's essay may, as I have suggested in a previous note, offer a 'way through' this difficulty. The fact may, nevertheless, remain that phenomenology will always prove insufficient to judge the difference between impersonal chaos and interpersonal indeterminacy. In so far as this observation harbours a question as to the intentionality of thought and the nature of intuition (not to mention their implications in transcendence), this may in turn suggest a root cause of the apparent oscillations of theology towards nihilism and of true nihilism towards theology.

48  *Radical Orthodoxy*, pp. 1-2.

impersonal chaos and the infinite indeterminacy of intra- and inter-personal harmonious order? How are we to distinguish between infinite and finite indeterminacies (whether of the finite or the infinite)? Between the void and the nothingness which has its place within the created order? Between the nothingness by which that order is punctuated and articulated, and the greater nothingness of disharmony (an analogy of 'nothing')? Between the dissonant nothingness of disharmony, the sweet silences and harmony of companionship, and the violent nothingnesses of the 'silence' and 'silencing' of the "politics of noise"?

(iii) "What sort of shadow? A reversal that would explode every perceptible proportion in the existential structures of mortal life?"[49] How are we to be reconciled to the Christian doctrine of reconciliation? How are we to come to terms with the fact that the catastrophe of the Cross is not simply intelligible, in that, whilst it most surely does ensure that violence is not the end without dealing with violence violently, its theological and Christological, indeed its cosmological, significance must nevertheless not be permitted to obscure its materiality, nor silence its genuinely sinister, violent reality?[50]

(iv) To what extent will any attempt to recover our lost sense of participation require not only exposition of a theology of participation and of a doctrine of analogy, but also a rigorous attention to a properly Christological doctrine of the analogy of participation, in which analogy and participation will be permitted to illumine each other, and which will not be falsely grounded in an absent and absenting (Body of) Christ – but rather grounded in and as an

---

49 *Radical Orthodoxy*, p. 139.
50 See footnote on "non-oppositional undoing of opposition" and Augustine's doctrine of the atonement above. This thus links the Christology and atonement in which God begins human music and time again, in time (*Radical Orthodoxy*, p. 269), directly to the cosmology in which substantiality is perpetually crossed out by the emergence of time. (*Radical Orthodoxy*, p. 248). This question also returns us to Rose's criticisms of an ecclesiology of mending and prompts the following inflection of the question here at stake: how is diremption to be redeemed? Which again, it must be said, simply has no simple answer, even in the cross and resurrection of Christ.

account of the relation between the ideal and the real in Christ? (This would amount, not least, to a reflection upon Balthasar's dangerous suggestion that Christ may be regarded as the "concrete *analogia entis*".[51])

(v) "Only transcendence, which 'suspends' these things [embodied life, self-expression, sexuality, aesthetic experience, human political community] in the sense of interrupting them, 'suspends' them also in the other sense of upholding their relative worth over-against the void."[52] Where, exactly, is the 'material' to be suspended – in thought; above the void; over-against the void; before God; in Christ? More specifically, what does Christological suspension *look* like?

51   Von Balthasar, H. U., *A Theology of History*, London, Sheed & Ward, 1963 (*Theologie der Geschichte*, Einsiedlen, Johannes Verlag, 1959) p. 69, note 5.
52   *Radical Orthodoxy*, p.3.

# PART V
# CONCLUSION

# Chapter Ten

# Conclusion:
# Continuing the Conversation

James Hanvey SJ

*I came upon a child of God*
*He was walking along the road*
*And I asked him, where are you going*
*And this he told me*
*I am going on down to Yasgur's farm*
*I'm going to join in a rock 'n' roll band*
*I'm going to camp out on the land*
*And try to get my soul free*
*We are stardust*
*We are golden*
*And we've got to get ourselves back to the garden*

*Woodstock* – Joni Mitchell

Radical Orthodoxy: what does it mean and what does it intend? The book that
bears this title clearly intends to launch a debate which raises questions about
the circumstances and possibilities of theology in the social and intellectual
culture of postmodernity. If the title is to be more than a mere publisher's
catch-phrase then it must entail a programme that not only offers an
interpretation of the theological enterprise thus far, but also sets out how that
enterprise may proceed. Indeed, part of the contention of the writers who
group themselves under this title is that the 'orthodoxy' they seek to retrieve
will prove to be radical. It offers theology a way out of the epistemological
and ontological impasse it has arrived at through too readily accepting
modernity's separation of faith and reason. Moreover, it is possible to harness

the insights of postmodernity's critique of modernity to create a new situation in which theologians may fruitfully recover themes which have been neglected, to the impoverishment of Christian life and its capacity to deal effectively with a profoundly secular culture, which nevertheless seeks a spirituality. To this extent, Radical Orthodoxy sees itself as a creative protest against the 'Sea of Faith' on the one hand, and a fervent evangelical fundamentalism on the other. It offers itself, therefore, as an alternative.

As it is presented, Radical Orthodoxy understands itself to be ecumenical. Although it arises within a particular Anglican debate, it does not intend to restrict itself to such parochial horizons. If its analysis is correct, then the epistemological, historical, and metaphysical issues and themes which it has identified must be pertinent to all Christian traditions that have a common intellectual and cultural European history. Indeed, the 'radical' and the 'orthodoxy' are determined to a large extent by the way the members of this group interpret that tradition. While this should alert us to the degree of self-positioning that is part of the undisclosed hermeneutics of these thinkers, it also directs us to their method of conversation as a mode of engagement. It is in that spirit of conversation that this essay is offered.

## Identifying the Task

The task that Radical Orthodoxy identifies for theology and sets as its own programme rests on a diagnosis of modernity and postmodernity. Its diagnosis is not especially original, for it sees modernity as the emergence of a secular consciousness which excludes God. It argues that the root of this lies in the differentiation of faith and reason, which consigns faith to a realm of personal belief and conviction, as opposed to reason which secures knowledge and truth. Not only is such a division disastrous for the possibility of theology, it also presents us with a profound metaphysical error, which ultimately leads to a false grasp of reality at best, and a paralysing nihilism at worst.[1] In the light of this Radical Orthodoxy proposes to heal this deadly

---

1   *Radical Orthodoxy*, London, Routledge, 1999, p.3.  See Milbank, J., *The Programme of Radical Orthodoxy* in this volume.

wound of modernity by overcoming the vicious separation and recovering an integral ontology with a corresponding theory of 'participation'.

This, of course, could be a secular programme, but for members of the group like Milbank and Pickstock it can only be accomplished by the return of God. They advocate a form of Neoplatonist strategy which they claim is central to the tradition, whereby all being, hence truth and knowledge, is grounded in the divine mind. In this way, reality is reclaimed, and with it the whole of Christian European history from which modernity has also alienated us by silencing the voices of tradition, especially those whose achievement resists the separation of faith and reason. If Radical Orthodoxy is correct, then it should be possible to reclaim these voices; hence the concern to revisit both the voices and the sites of the tradition. In accomplishing this task Radical Orthodoxy offers another 'story' that claims to be yet another (more truthful?) version of modernity.[2]

Radical Orthodoxy has much in common with many theologians who have also tried to respond to the questions modernity poses for theology, by offering a critique of modernity itself.[3] Where Radical Orthodoxy claims a difference is in its acceptance of a critique offered by postmodern thinkers, while using some of the insights and methods developed by them. It correctly perceives the significance of this postmodern critique for the whole intellectual and cultural enterprise, and recognises that it offers theology new potentials in language and conceptuality, especially in unmasking the assumptions and strategies of modernity in which theology has acquiesced. It would not, however, agree with the more radical anti-foundationalist positions of many postmodern thinkers. Insofar as Radical Orthodoxy attempts to be a mediating position, it presents a stimulus to the work of constructing theological discourse in a significantly changed cultural environment. Yet it also points to a dilemma in the programme: if the postmodern critique of modernity is accepted as largely correct, how can theology continue, without constructing for itself a pre-modern position which

---

2 Milbank, J., *The Programme of Radical Orthodoxy*, p. 38.
3 See, for example, Placher, W. C., *The Domestication of Transcendence: How modern Thinking About God Went Wrong*, Kentucky, Westminster John Knox Press, 1996; Dupré, L., *Passage to Modernity: An Essay in the Hermeneutics of Nature and Culture*, New Haven, Yale University Press, 1993.

opens it to the charge of nostalgia; how can it establish a theological foundationalism which can withstand both the critique of modernity and postmodernity?

These are questions to which we shall return, but it suffices here to illuminate the project Radical Orthodoxy sets for itself. The project intends to be more than a mere therapeutic exercise. It has quite extensive soteriological pretensions; the healing of a broken epistemology, through the construction of an ontology that can ground knowledge and faith, thereby restoring coherence and authority to a fragmented and marginalised Christian discourse. It is a magisterial project that seeks legitimisation not only in its results, but also by enlisting the authoritative voices of the past that Radical Orthodoxy claims now to interpret correctly. By relocating these voices within Radical Orthodoxy, it also makes implicit claims to save them from "the time of error" marked by the late Middle Ages, The Reformation, and The Enlightenment.[4] At times Radical Orthodoxy seems to see itself as an intellectual Noah's Ark, in which we may safely float upon the floods of nihilism and ontological disintegration until they recede.

On the positive side, Radical Orthodoxy is surely correct in reminding us that theology can never settle for a simple separation or differentiation of the spheres of faith and knowledge. The task of theology is not something its creates for itself, but something that it understands to be given by the event of revelation. This event, by its very nature, challenges the dualism of divine/human, sacred/secular, nature/grace, knowledge/faith, and so on, and calls theology to attend to the relationship which is disclosed. It is this relationship which requires a new conceptuality, hence a new understanding of being, truth, and knowledge. It is the struggle to attend to, and articulate, the nature of this relationship, and the God who is disclosed in and through it, that forces theology to the adventure of thought and speech. We can trace this in the great 'quantum leap' of Trinitarian thought, forged in the struggle with the conservative rationalism of Arianism. Theology, at its best, shows itself to be attentive to the thought and culture of its time, but in fidelity to its task it is also critical, radical, and innovative.

4    Milbank, J., *The Programme of Radical Orthodoxy*, p. 44.

In the case of Trinitarian orthodoxy, not only was a radically new conceptuality for speaking and thinking about God fashioned, but a new way of understanding humanity and the created order was also forged. Theology knows that it can never be just talk about God, but must always be 'human talk' about God. This means that it must always be engaged upon the work of interpreting the human sphere in order that in and through that sphere it can speak rationally and truthfully of God, as God has given God's self to be known and spoken of. Theology is an always new event of speech, that must test its own truth by constantly offering to humanity an understanding of what it is to be human, an understanding that is more coherent and generative than anything humanity can devise for itself. Without this critical attention and self-awareness, theology is always in danger of becoming a private language that betrays its own logic, at best a dead rhetoric, or vague spirituality that seeks to articulate the longing for transcendence. Radical Orthodoxy is aware of the task and the danger, and so makes a claim for a serious consideration of the strategy it proposes, and the alternative it constructs. It is to this consideration that we now turn.

## Strategy

### *Not Nostalgia*

As a phenomenon of postmodern culture, nostalgia is a manifestation of a deracination of both the self and culture. It arises from a deep sense of displacement, or dis-ease, with the present, and an inability to trust the future. There may well be a lurking awareness of nihilism which marks modernity. The strategy is to 'get ourselves back to the garden' and this entails the construction of a 'past' which can be inhabited. Given that such a 'past' is our construction and we control it, we can be assured that it is secure. Nostalgia is a form of escape in which there is a willing suspension of our suspicion. It is not constructed out of any historical accuracy, but out of an emotional imagination, a creation that derives from our anxieties, and our need to relieve them in a place of safety and psychic warmth. Of course, such a strategy is an admission of failure, the song of an exile that has abandoned hope and therefore reconstructs an ideal homeland or Eden. This strategy is, at bottom, not a response to the challenge of nihilism, but surrender to it. Some critics have detected this strategy of nostalgia in Radical Orthodoxy and leading members of its circle.[5] They understand its attempts to redraw the relationship between faith and reason, and the subsequent reinstatement of a theologically driven metaphysics with claims to absolutism, as a return to a naïve pre-modernity. Far from overcoming modernity and responding to the aporia of postmodernity, Radical Orthodoxy is itself the product of postmodernity and a victim of its radical resistance to any totalising foundationalist claims.

As Radical Orthodoxy understands and presents itself, it does not advocate a strategy of nostalgia and it would be a mistake to read it in this way. To be sure, it is critical of the epistemology of modernity, but it intends no mere reconstruction of an ideal age; rather, it seeks to provide a new synthesis which is based on three moments: (a) the refusal to settle for fideism; (b) or to collude with modernity; (c) but to reconstruct an ontology and epistemology on the basis of the beatific vision. Sometimes this is argued in terms of an Augustinian 'ontological peace' but more circumspectly it is presented in terms of the goal of all human knowing. It is a foundational principle which grounds human knowing in the divine mind so that our knowing of what there is, is a participation in the divine knowing. If the postmodern critique exposes the assumptions of modernity such that we can no longer work with them, then the only way forward is not to reconstruct 'the' past, but through an engagement with those pre-modern thinkers who mapped the Christian vision of reality. It is in this way that we may begin to rediscover how that reality may be grasped once more.

In his contribution to this volume, John Milbank seeks to locate this strategy and defend it. On the one hand, he distinguishes it from the neo-orthodoxy of Karl Barth; on the other, he argues for his substantial agreement with the Catholic movement of *la nouvelle théologie*. However, he

5   Lakeland, P., *Postmodernity*, Minneapolis, Fortress Press, 1997, p. 43. See especially pp.68-76 for Lakeland's sustained objections to Milbank's "countermodernity". See also Roberts, R. H., *Transcendental Sociology?* (review article) in *The Journal of Scottish Theology*, October 1993, Vol. 46. No. 4. Roberts argues that Milbank's thesis in *Theology and Social Theory*, Oxford, Blackwell, 1990, forces theology to become "the imposition of stasis, a rearward-looking construal", "an extended and brilliant exercise in despair".

differentiates himself from the latter movement, charging that it "colludes with a modernity that it helps to construct". Radical Orthodoxy as a programme is therefore to understand itself, he says, as refuting any dualism of the sacred/secular so that instead it reclaims or redeems an ontological, epistemological, and social, wholeness.

It is difficult to assess the weight of these alleged distinctions and criticisms, especially as it is precisely the achievement of *la nouvelle théologie* that it overcomes an oppositional, but not contrastive, sacred/secular dualism. Indeed, it is the way in which Radical Orthodoxy seeks to locate itself, and to establish its critical and constructive claims *against* those with whom it might otherwise be thought to want most closely to collaborate, that begins to alert us to its own strategy of deception. Given that it understands itself to be uniquely undeceived, and argues its *via media* not through constructive analysis and argument but by a serious of counterclaims, it is in danger of generating a huge rhetorical edifice, itself a monument to the failure of imagination that marks the postmodern. It may be useful therefore to bring it into a less passive conversation with Barth and Catholic thought.

## Not Barth

It is difficult to see how the claims Milbank makes could support anything other than a superficial reading of Karl Barth's theology. He is surely correct in understanding Barth's starting point as rooted in Kantian epistemology and the questions posed in the 19th century concerning the ground of our knowledge of God and the nature of faith. However, he fails to see that Barth not only engages in a critique of these positions but also moves far beyond them. The whole of the *Church Dogmatics* entails a sustained rejection of the presuppositions of modernity without collapsing into a fideism. This is the point of Barth's work on Anselm[6] and the section of *Church Dogmatics* where he works through the whole problem of Kantian epistemology, and its

---

6 Barth, K., *Gesamtausgabe*, Vol. 13, *Fides quærens intellectum*, Zürich, Theologischer Verlag, 1981 (1931), translated by Robertson, I. W. as *Anselm: Fides Quærens Intellectum*, London, SCM, 1960.

deficiency in the light of revelation.[7] Far from accepting it as the only word about human reason, Barth is clear that the word of reason is always a deficient word. Barth, in distinction to Milbank, does not accept Kant's presuppositions, but rather exposes them in such a way as to illustrate that there is precisely no autonomous space for reason and faith – this is itself a distortion of reason.

Without such a foundational analysis Barth could not sustain his innovative reworking of the doctrine of God and his narrative theology of the Trinity. The effect of both these moves is to generate a dynamic ontology which thoroughly places God as the principle subject of human history, grounded in God's own act of revelation. It is from this perspective that Barth might argue that it is Radical Orthodoxy, at least as it is presented by John Milbank, that has succumbed to the assumptions of modernity. What otherwise does Milbank mean, for instance, by "pure faith, pure unanticipated revelation over against reason"?[8] This is not the sum of Barth's dialectical logic, but rather represents the way Barth might be caricatured if he were read with certain assumptions about faith and reason, and without attending to how he rules such a position out.

---

7    Barth, K., *Studiensausgabe*, Vol. 11 *Die kirkliche Dogmatik*, Vol. 2, *Die Lehre von Gott, 1*, Zürich, Theologischer Verlag, 1988. Translated and edited by Bromiley G. W. and Torrance T. F. as *Church Dogmatics*, Vol. 2.1, *The Doctrine of God*, Edinburgh, T & T Clark, 1956. Particularly relevant is the dialectical argument between the two parts of §26: *The Knowability of God*. This is further developed in §27.2: *The Veracity of Man's Knowledge*. Barth's lectures, published as *Schicksal und Idee* (Barth, K., *Theologische Fragen und Antworten*, Zollikon, Evangelischer Verlag, 1957), provide an important context for this discussion. Of course, the ground was prepared in *Die kirkliche Dogmatik*, Zürich,Theologischer Verlag, 1988, Vol. I, 1, pp. 25-34 (Translated and edited by Bromiley G. W. and Torrance, T. F. as *Church Dogmatics*, Edinburgh, T & T Clark, 1975 [1960]), with Barth's criticism of Schleiermacher and Hermann, the philosophies of dualism and immanence, and Catholic attempts at an *a priori* ontology. For Barth, there was more at issue than mere academic disputation, for he saw these moves as having disastrous political implications. Cf. Barth, K., *Theologische Existenz Heute*, Munich, Kaiser Verlag, 1984 (1933), Vol. 2, *Zwischen den Zeiten*. Although Barth is concerned to reject what he understands (incorrectly) to be the Catholic notion of *analogia entis* in favour of *analogia fidei*, he nevertheless has much in common with Aquinas in his understanding of the epistemological status of faith.

8    Milbank, J., *The Programme of Radical Orthodoxy*, p. 34.

Barth's position is not as dualistic as many have conceived it to be; rather, he denies that an autonomous human reason can attain to any saving knowledge of God, for that would make God's revelation redundant. It would also falsify the actual situation of human reason before the revelation which exposes it as fallen. Reason too needs to be redeemed.

Likewise, is it not precisely Barth's point that there can be no secure reason other than as grounded in God's truth about himself, about our world and about us? What can it mean to say that in order to speak about God we must speak about something else?[9] Milbank seems to argue this out of a fallen world which can only have an "anticipated vision of the divine" and therefore is reduced to "a figurative anticipation of the incarnate logos".[10] From the position of the *Church Dogmatics*, however, it would seem that Radical Orthodoxy has substituted a notion of the 'beatific vision' for revelation, and has in some way chosen to bypass the significance of Jesus Christ for the sake of a Mediæval construct (which in its origins did not make sense without him). In fact, 'the argument from the beatific vision' seems to make of knowledge an eschatological reality. Is this sustainable either within the context of Mediæval thought, or within the critical realism that marks the practice of our daily experience? Does it represent the hidden desperation of one who has accepted too easily a postmodern anti-foundationalist critique? There is a deep incoherence of Radical Orthodoxy's epistemological claims on the one hand, whilst on the other its exponents seem to have succumbed to a postmodern understanding of the possibilities of modernity. Is this not a 'double bluff'?

Finally, a reader schooled in the *Church Dogmatics* may wish to ask simply, quietly, and peaceably of these sophisticated Thebans: has not God revealed himself in his Word, Jesus Christ, and thus given us the possibility of knowledge and true speech about himself? Moreover, is not the unfolding of the reality of God, as the one who loves in freedom, the very basis of theology's own freedom; the act that establishes it as the immanent critique of culture on the one hand, and an inexhaustible redemptive generativity of human culture on the other? If Radical Orthodoxy cared to respond to the

---

9 Milbank, J., *The Programme of Radical Orthodoxy*, p. 34.
10 Milbank, J., *The Programme of Radical Orthodoxy*, p. 34.

questions I have posed here, it would do well to consider the charges it makes against Barth. The issues here concern not only accuracy, but also the apparent lack of depth of Radical Orthodoxy's knowledge of Barth's texts, a lack which threatens to expose the inadequacies and pre-judgements of Radical Orthodoxy's own position.

## Not Catholic Transcendentalism

If it seeks to position itself at some distance from a version of 'Barthianism', Radical Orthodoxy has been keen to locate its closeness to recent Catholic thought, especially the Catholic *nouvelle théologie*. It is prepared to make the astonishing claim that Henri de Lubac, as a central figure in this movement, was "a greater theological revolutionary than Karl Barth".[11] Milbank seems to confuse de Lubac's Augustinianism, underpinned by Blondel, with his own position on Aquinas. From this he proceeds to approve de Lubac as the inaugurator of postmodern theology.

Even though de Lubac is awarded a place in the pantheon of Radical Orthodoxy's heroes, he, or at least his legacy in Catholicism, is assessed as guilty of collusion with modernity. "Collusion" is, of course, a pejorative term in the rhetorical arsenal of Radical Orthodoxy.[12] To a large extent it is correct to perceive that the influential and formative theology of theologians like de Lubac and Congar is in an intense debate with modernity. However, their perceptiveness obscures the strategy of the theology they develop and prevents Radical Orthodoxy from hearing the questions it may also put to them.

11 Milbank, J., *The Programme of Radical Orthodoxy*, p. 35.
12 Milbank, J., *The Programme of Radical Orthodoxy*, p. 33. There seems to be a series of confusions about de Lubac and his legacy in Catholic thought. It is surely one of de Lubac's achievements that he does create a 'common human rational discourse and foundation for theology' in such a way that it is not a relativisation of the Church's influence. As de Lubac himself remarks of *Surnaturel* (Paris, Aubier, 1946) it was "a sort of effort to re-establish contact between Catholic theology and contemporary thought, or at least to eliminate one basic obstacle to that contact, not for the sake of some 'adaptation' to that thought, but rather to enable dialogue with it" (*Mémoire sur l'occasion de mes écrits*, Namur, Culture et Vérité, 1989, p. 34 f.). In the light of de Lubac's own self-understanding it is difficult to corroborate Milbank's objection.

Like Radical Orthodoxy, *la nouvelle théologie* as a movement was concerned with the relation between nature and grace, and the way in which this relation reflects and determines the relation between faith and reason. Their strategy was one of retrieval, focused on those masters of discourse who had been foundational for the Church, especially Augustine and Aquinas.[13] They sought to free their thought from a deadening scholasticism, underpinned by an ahistorical theology of tradition developed by Kleutgen, itself reinforced by the dominance of the Roman school under Franzelin and his successor Palmieri.[14] It was a bold and subtle strategy, especially as it had much in common with the Modernist movement condemned by Pope Pius X in 1907. In its retrieval of the tradition it was inspired by the thought of Maurice Blondel, his rejection of extrinsicism, and the 'method of immanence' developed in his work (especially *L'Action*[15]). Following this method this movement brought Augustine and Aquinas into dialogue with modernity in such a way that the dynamism of their thought, and *la nouvelle théologie*'s

---

13 Although Augustine and Aquinas constitute the major voices because of the enormous influence they had had in the Church, especially in the formative debates over grace and nature in Jansenism, and faith and reason at Vatican I, considerable attention was also paid to the thought of Origen, as well as 19th Century theologians such as Möhler and Scheeban. Newman was also important to the French school, not only for his treatment of the existential and epistemological structure of faith, but because of his theory of development and its implicit theology of history in the life of the Church. The place Newman gives to the faith of the laity as a theological resource was particularly interesting for Congar, as he sought to develop his own theology of the laity (Congar, Y., *Jalons pour une théologie du laïcat*, Paris, Éditions du Cerf, 1954, translated by Attwater, D., as *Lay People in the Church: A Study for A Theology of Laity*, London, Bloomsbury, 1957).

14 See, for a fuller description of Kleutgen and his school, Deufel, K., *Kirche und Tradition: ein Beitrag zur Geschichte der theologischen Wende im 19. Jahrhundert am Beispiel des kirchlich-theologischen Kampfprogramms Joseph Kleutgens: Darstellung und neue Quellen*, Munich, Schoningh, 1976. For the style of interpretation at work in this school of Thomism, see for example, Franzelin, J.-B., *Tractatus de Verbo Incarnato*, Rome, Tata Giovanni, 1902.

15 Blondel, M., *L'Action*, Paris, F. Alcan, 1936-7 (2 Vols.). Cf. also de Lubac's short but significant essay, *The Conditions of Ontological Affirmation as Set Forth in L'Action by Maurice Blondel* in *Theological Fragments*, San Francisco, Ignatius, 1989 (translated from *Théologies d'occasion* Paris, Desclée de Brouwer, 1984), especially pp. 388-392. This is especially interesting, given that de Lubac's own teacher was Pedro Descoqs, whose view had been opposed to Blondel and whose position was strongly Suárezian.

synthesis of grace and nature (with its corresponding re-conceptualisation of metaphysics), could be applied to the questions it posed.

The point was not to create a pre-modern world, or indeed, reinforce an ecclesial ghetto: but to break out of it by mapping a dynamic humanism that is, *per essentiam*, open to, and constituted in, its relation to God.[16] Far from being exiled by the Enlightenment, Christian revelation is the only way in which reason can fulfil its intellectual, human, social, and cultural goal. Modernity rightly grasps the possibilities, the *telos,* of human nature. Its flaw is in constituting the 'self' and its powers alone as a valid soteriology.

The strategy was not to abandon the Cartesian self (or subject), but to reclaim that self as the *imago Dei*, thereby showing that the self exists, knows, and acts, out of the dynamic transcendence which is grace. In other words, in the very act of grasping 'the self', the subject must also grasp the relationship which grounds it: God as such. From this base, Christianity is seen to nourish a profound, creative, and universal humanism, and to establish an irreducible solidarity between all persons by virtue of their constitution and *telos*, and to abolish the vitiating dualism of nature/grace as if they operated as two opposed orders. The strategy finds its most complete and rigorous application in the fundamental theologies of Karl Rahner and Bernard Lonergan. The effect is to furnish the Church with a powerful synthetic conceptuality that strengthens its engagement with modernity. It also entrusts to the community of faith a renewed understanding of itself as the true home of humanity, thereby redrawing the battlelines between the Church and modern/postmodern culture. In rejecting the dualism of sacred/secular, this 'new' theology was able to reclaim every aspect of human life as the realm of encounter with grace – the 'ordinary' may now be understood and experienced as sacrament. This has had an effect upon Catholic practice which has yet fully to be appreciated and evaluated.[17]

16  This is the central thesis of de Lubac's *De la Connaissance de Dieu*, Paris, Éditions de Témoignage, 1941, esp. pp. 57-61. *Connaissance* was greatly expanded in *Sur les Chemins de Dieu*, Paris, Aubier, 1956. The theme of both works is developed in a more systematic and philosophical way by Karl Rahner and Bernard Lonergan.

17  One significant aspect is the understanding of mysticism and its possibility as an 'ordinary' grounding experience. Cf. Karl Rahner, *Experience of Self and Experience of God* in *Theological Investigations*, London, Darton, Longman, and Todd, 1975, Vol. 13. For a wider discussion and context Cf. Bernard McGinn, *Theoretical Foundations* (Appendix)

Milbank is, therefore, correct in identifying the most significant and influential forms of Catholic theology up to the Council as accepting the position represented by modernity.[18] However, the strategy he criticises may in turn question his own assumptions. If the position of *la nouvelle théologie* is correct, and there is an integral relation between nature and grace, faith and reason, then it follows that all human intellectual achievement must carry the reality of this relation, even when it rejects it, or is unconscious of it. Under this logic, a Catholic appeal to metaphysics is required, under pain of self-contradiction, to look for the 'good' in modernity and to recognise that it can and will speak truly, albeit partially.[19] Thus, this very principle which a Catholic sensibility is concerned to defend prevents it from rejecting what has preceded, and commits it to a discerning, positive, hermeneutic which is profoundly humane. It rejects a view of history as an either/or, ante/post; but precisely on the basis of an understanding of grace as integral to the essence of being human. History is grasped as continuity, or narrative of the *desiderium* from which it receives its inner dynamism. As de Lubac's *Catholicisme* illustrates, it is this principle which gives Catholicism its profound Christian humanism, universalism, and inclusivist instincts.[20] Modernism may be incomplete and flawed, but it also possesses important truths which are significant for theology; indeed, which are necessary, if

in *The Presence of God: Theoretical Approaches*, New York, Crossroads, 1991, Vol. 1.

18 It is also important within Catholic thought to appreciate the achievement of thinkers like de Lubac and Congar and the nature of their strategy of engagement with modernity. Their own thought is now in the process of 'retrieval' by conservative movements uneasy with developments within the Catholic Church since Vatican II. It is necessary to distinguish *ressourcement* from *restoration*.

19 In this regard work of Helmut Peukert, and his critique and development of the thought of Jürgen Habermas, furnishes an interesting enrichment of theology in debate with modernity. Cf. *Enlightenment and Theology as Unfinished Projects,* especially pp. 56-62 in Browning, D. S. and Schüssler Fiorenza, F., Eds., *Habermas, Modernity and Public Theology*, New York, Crossroads, 1992; also the more extensive development of his thesis in Peukert, H., *Wissenschaftstheorie, Handlungstheorie, fundamentale Theologie*, Dusseldorf, Patmos Verlag, 1976, translated by Bohman, J., as *Science, Action, and Fundamental Theology*, Massachusetts, MIT Press, 1984.

20 De Lubac, H., *Catholicisme: les aspects sociaux du dogme*, Paris, Éditions du Cerf, 1947. Translated as *Catholicism: A Study of Dogma in Relation to the Corporate Destiny of Mankind*, London, Burnes & Oates, 1950.

theology itself is to be self-critical and alert to its own partiality. Modernism may lead to nihilism, but not inevitably. Where it can establish itself in an understanding of the human self, and in knowledge as grounded in a transcendental dynamic ordered to the source of being and truth, then it can see itself as a graced movement; part of the unfolding of human redemption and becoming.[21]

Surely the epistemology advocated by Radical Orthodoxy must commit it to the same understanding? It is in posing this question that one becomes aware of the gaps in Radical Orthodoxy: its failure to substantiate its epistemology other than by asserting it; its absence of any theology of the human person; and the absence of a coherent hermeneutic of history. It is simply not good enough to claim that modernity is a bad thing, and that every thinker before Radical Orthodoxy is in need of rescue, without presenting a theology that can coherently deal with modernity's criticisms.

If Radical Orthodoxy has a fear of "colluding" with modernity, is there not a danger that it colludes with postmodernity? If postmodernity has successfully exposed the claims of modernity, and can sustain its attack on foundationalism and maintain its method of resistance, why should it accept the even greater ontological and epistemological claims of Radical Orthodoxy? Claims to ground human knowledge through a participation in the divine mind must sound no more convincing to a postmodern culture than the claims of the Enlightenment do to members of Radical Orthodoxy. Indeed, why should we subscribe to a deeply problematic quasi-mythological

---

21  Even if one does accept that modernity masks a nihilism, Laurence Hemming's suggestive essay *Nihilism: Heidegger and the Grounds of Redemption,* (*Radical Orthodoxy*, pp. 91-108) proposes an approach which seems to run counter to other thinkers in the group. It is a strategy with affinities to the one we have been sketching from other Catholic authors. Rather than signal the end of theology, the emergence of nihilism in modernity may offer a new space for encounter with God (p. 103), offering a sense of self as given: "God comes to me as a way of making me who I am. As I speak in a Godly way, God comes to me *as* me, *with* me, revealed *in* me". Hemming's thesis is suggestive of the line taken by Xavier Zubiri, *El Hombre y Dios*, Madrid, Alianza: Sociedad de Estudios y Publicaciones, 1985, pp. 318-328. Zubiri says: "Recibe el hombre justamente esta donación en forma de un 'hacia' y no pura y simplemente como algo que está delante nosotros. La experiencia de Dios es una experiencia real, a parte Dei, porque es real donación experiencial. En el hecho de constituirse el hombre como una persona principalmente absoluta, Dios se da como experienciable, como fundamento experiencial y experienciable y experienciado".

platonic metaphysics and that strange invention of 'the divine mind'? Surely the postmodern critique of all metaphysics and meta-narratives applies here too, asking the same questions about the claims to truth masking a claim to power.

Even if Radical Orthodoxy attempts to avoid these questions through a series of occasional performative demonstrations, the return to postmodern sites (such as the body, space, language, and so forth) remains only a series of improvisations upon postmodern themes.[22] This contradicts Radical Orthodoxy's foundationalist claims. For all its provocative and stimulating conversation, I am, therefore, left wondering how it can sustain its coherence.

## Hermeneutics

If the attempts of Radical Orthodoxy to position itself with regard to Barth and European Catholic thought have raised important questions about the sustainability of its judgment and strategy, the very questions they have provoked point the way to the theological tasks that still have to be accomplished. It is important that the insights of the group should not be lost. Radical Orthodoxy's hermeneutics, for example, are worthy of closer attention. This may be approached in the two ways I now want to examine.

The first concerns the obvious but important point that Radical Orthodoxy operates with a 'pre-judgment' in Gadamer's sense.[23] It comes to analyse modernity with a view that must result in its diagnosis of nihilism, whose cause, it claims, lies ultimately in its separation of faith and reason. This judgment further guides the texts it selects to retrieve as illustrations of the synthesis of faith, reason, and praxis, in retrievals that it recommends as antidote to the current situation. Radical Orthodoxy imposes a continuity of judgment and metaphysics upon the texts selected, consequently forcing them to speak within the same perspective as that of the group. In turn, this generates a naïve, strangely de-historicised and de-contextualised, appropriation of the texts concerned.

22  Cf. *Radical Orthodoxy*, p. 3.
23  Gadamer, H.-G., *Wahrheit und Methode*, Tübingen, Mohr, 1960, p. 254 f. Translated as *Truth and Method*, London, Sheed & Ward, 1979 (1975), p. 239 f.

In Radical Orthodoxy's treatment of Aquinas, for example, there seems little awareness of the principal schools of Thomistic hermeneutics that have emerged in this century, and within which Radical Orthodoxy is itself operating.[24] The effect is to assume that a practitioner of Radical Orthodoxy is somehow an uncontaminated, and therefore authentic, expositor (as opposed to interpreter) of the text, because the practitioner shares the same fundamental perspective held by the author of the text. The problems connected with this hermeneutical circle are obvious: under the guise of retrieval there is appropriation or, to use a more postmodern concept, colonisation. History is here revealed as inherently collapsible because the 'true intention', both of author and practitioner, are underpinned by what they retrieve: God.

The problem is not irremediable; not only is there a requirement that attention be given to the cultural contexts of the text *and* the practitioner, but also recognition of the difference between them. We know that the Plato before Christ is not the same as the Plato of Augustine, or Renaissance Humanism, or the 20th Century, yet the importance of this obvious point lies in its respect for history and for revelation.[25] It is essential to the generativity of all theology that it can attend to the particular and the different voice. It is this recognition and support of distinction and the different voice that allows it to be a genuine conversation; a community of perspectives and insights,

---

24 These may be characterised as participationist, transcendental, and analogical. The transcendentalist approach has been most influential through the work of Maréchal, Rahner and Lonergan as we noted above. In its epistemological claims Radical Orthodoxy seems to come closest to this approach, though, as I have pointed out, it lacks the philosophical depth and coherence of these theologians. Of more interest to Radical Orthodoxy, the participationist approach represented by Fabro, Geiger, Montagnes and especially de Raeymaeker L., whose work, *Philosophie de l'être: Essai de synthèse métaphysique* (Louvain, Institut supérieur de philosophie, 1947, translated by Ziegelmayer, E. H., as *The Philosophy of Being: A synthesis of Metaphysics*, St. Louis, Herder, 1954), already accomplishes much of the synthesis Radical Orthodoxy seeks. In a complementary way, the works of G. Klubertanz, R. McInerny and B. Mondin on notions of 'analogy' and participation in Aquinas are also relevant.

25 It is part of the argument developed in Sokolowski, R., *The God of Faith and Reason: The Foundations of Christian Theology*, Indiana, University of Notre Dame Press, 1982, that revelation grounds Christian distinctness and gives rise to its distinct voices. These are not antithetical to the natural order or to human reason, but create the distance, or difference, in which mystery emerges without presenting itself as incoherence. See, in particular, p. 37.

without reducing them to the one voice or hegemony of a specific period or movement. If, as both Milbank and Pickstock assert, "time [is] ... eternity's moving image"[26] it would seem that this becomes a difficult, if even not redundant, task, especially if the interpreter claims the privilege of speaking from the perspective of 'eternity'. We may note, in passing, that this also applies to the exercise of any magisterial authority within a community. If it is to be a genuine guarantor of revelation and continuity to tradition, then it must protect and nurture the distinctive voices that manifest the Spirit.

The other effect is to overlook, or smooth out, the real tensions and questions which may exist in a theologian's work in enlisting them to our cause.[27] For example, Radical Orthodoxy's approach to Aquinas may present his understanding of faith and reason as less problematic than it really is. Indeed, it is part of de Lubac's argument in *Surnaturel* that Aquinas' thought contains a basic instability, which later ages would exploit with unfortunate consequences.[28] One careful commentator on Aquinas' work alerts us to a paradox in his theology which Radical Orthodoxy seems inclined to ignore:

> ... one is quite hard-pressed to find any theologians in history so emphatically committed to the origin of all truth in the One God, as so vigorously confident that the *lumen fidei* can enrich, guide, transform, and intensify on a new level the entire range of natural reason. Yet, on the other hand, one would be equally hard-pressed to find any theologian in history so radically aware of the infinite distance between God and creature, and so utterly insistent that the essence of the Triune God remains absolutely shrouded in darkness during the sojourn *in via*.[29]

---

26 Pickstock, C., *Radical Orthodoxy and the Mediations of Time* in this volume, p. 64; cf. also Milbank, J., *The Programme of Radical Orthodoxy*, p. 42; and the *Introduction* to *Radical Orthodoxy*, p. 10.

27 Cf. Nicholas Lash's criticisms of John Milbank's interpretation of Aquinas in Lash, N., *Where Does Holy Teaching Leave Theology? Questions on Milbank's Aquinas* in *Modern Theology*, October 1999, Vol. 15, No. 4.

28 De Lubac, H., *Surnaturel*, p. 435 f.

29 Hall, D. C., *An Analysis of St. Thomas Aquinas' Expositio of the de Trinitate of Boethius*, Leiden, E. J. Brill, 1992, p. 122. Cf. also Donohoo, L. J., *The Nature and Grace of Sacra Doctrina in St. Thomas's Super Boëtium de Trinitate* in *The Thomist*, October 1999, Vol. 63, No. 4, especially pp. 351-358.

Indeed, it is arguable that the emphasis Radical Orthodoxy places upon the beatific vision as an epistemological ground and participationist paradigm of our knowing can deliver the system that is required. Aquinas is quite clear that, even in the beatified state, God is not attained as an object, but always remains a subject within human intentionality. The human intellect returns to itself, to see something of the divine *lumen* in its own operations. We never have knowledge of God *in se* but only through the graced relation that is given to us in faith.[30] In this regard, Aquinas arrives at a similar conclusion to Augustine's in *de Trinitate*.[31]

The second of these two hermeneutical ways concerns the claim that modernity leads to nihilism. In this case, Nietzsche seems to be a figure with whom Radical Orthodoxy has yet to come to terms. For Nietzsche, nihilism occurs when the highest values devalue themselves, a situation arrived at when "the aim or purpose is lacking and 'why?' can find no answer".[32] In *The Will to Power* he argues that nihilism is the end of meaning, and "the world looks valueless".[33] However, if we are content to stop at this point and accept the pessimism of this conclusion, then we are still suffering from reason's hangover – that the notions of 'purpose' and 'purposelessness' share the same presupposition of a network of causal connections. Nihilism, on the other hand, does not necessarily lead to meaninglessness; rather, it can act as a knife with which to cut the Gordian knot of reason that binds us. In nihilism we discover the freedom to be self-creating, for we are no longer caught in the

---

30  Cf. Aquinas, *Summa Theologiæ*, I. 1, Q. 12, a. 2, *Utrum Essentia Dei ab Intellectus Creato per Aliquam Similitudinem Vedeatur.*

31  Augustine, *de Trinitate*, Book 15, 7-11. Of particular note is Augustine's development of the idea of the 'imago Dei' while struggling to maintain the tension of our infinite unlikeness to God even when we possess God in eternity.

32  "Was bedeutet Nihilismus? – *Daß die obersten Werte sich entwerten. Es fehlt das Ziel; es fehlt die Antwort auf das 'Warum?'*" Nietzsche, F., *Der Wille zur Macht*, Stuttgart, Kröner Verlag, 1964 (1887), §2 (author's emphasis).

33  Nietzsche, F., *Der Wille zur Macht*, §12. Under the figure of the tightrope walker and the clown, the tension between a pessimistic nihilism, one that is still caught in the illusions of rationalism, and the creative nihilism, that with which the 'artist' works is further developed in *Zarathustra*. The artist is not the painter or musician as such, but the one who is free of illusion and therefore free to create his own value. (See Nietzsche, F., *Also Sprach Zarathustra: Von den drei Verwandlungen*, Frankfurt, Insel Verlag, 1994, p. 29 ff. Cf. also Eagleton, T., *The Ideology of the Aesthetic*, Oxford, Blackwell, 1990, pp. 256-259.

illusion of some pre-existing ontology. Hence the emergence of the figure of the 'artist'.[34] 'Meaning' is neither more or less than what the strong decide meaning shall be:

> To redeem the past and to transform every 'It was' into an 'I wanted it thus!' – that alone do I call redemption.[35]

Of course, this becomes an important weapon in the hands of a thinker like Foucault, who uses it to unmask the pretensions to reason and truth that inform modernity and its cultural institutions. We have already noted Radical Orthodoxy's weakness in dealing with a postmodern critique that may be brought to bear against its own claims, but from this perspective could it not be argued that its implicit hermeneutics is really the will to power? In fact, far from addressing modernity's nihilism, Radical Orthodoxy depends upon it. If this argument could be sustained against the programme of Radical Orthodoxy, it would mean that it had not escaped from the subject/object epistemology that characterises modernity; rather, its hermeneutics transposes it into a relationship of power. 'God' is constantly converted into an object and claimed as a convenient site or space from which to construct Radical Orthodoxy's edifice, 'a consumable fiction'. The appropriation of 'radical' and 'orthodox' are implicit claims to truth and authority which are simultaneously exposed as claims to power.

## Continuing the Conversation

Theology is speech about God. Each time theology speaks it must wrestle with the impossibility of its own act. Out of this wrestling comes an extraordinarily creative paradox: theology must constantly seek ways of

---

34  "Einen neuen Stolz lehrte mich mein Ich, den lehre ich die Menschen: nicht mehr den Kopf in den Sand der himmlischen Dinge zu stecken, sondern frei ihn zu tragen, einen Erden-Kopf, der der Erde Sinn schafft!" Nietzsche, F., *Also Sprach Zarathustra: Von den Hinterweltlern*, p. 35.
35  "Die Vergangenen zu erlösen und alles 'Es war' umzuschaffen in ein 'So wollte ich es!' – das hieße mir erst Erlösung." Nietzsche, F., *Also Sprach Zarathustra: Von der Erlösung*, p. 142.

speaking that which cannot be spoken; it must create a language which refers, by acknowledging that it cannot make of God an object. If postmodernity has freed us from the claims of modernity, it should not leave us disenchanted, but should provide a new impetus and context for theology to recovery its purpose.[36]

Radical Orthodoxy is an adventure that has barely begun. It has the time and resources to accomplish its task and respond to its critics. It can do this if it is prepared to return to the eternally generative problem of theology: that is, how to speak? I would venture to suggest that this task is not the constant recovery of texts, but rather the rediscovery of the one *single* task that gives theology all the resources and creativity it needs to engage the culture it faces. It is attention to this fundamental task which we find in Augustine and Aquinas, Barth and de Lubac, and which makes of them 'founders of discursivity'. It is a task described and charted by Gregory of Nazianzus[37] and Gregory of Nyssa: "How can we speak the name that is above every name?"[38] Yet, the discovery of this task does not plunge the discoverer into an apophatic silence; rather, it is the means by which God comes to be in speech. The reality in whose presence we are, surpasses, by the very nature of its reality, the power of customary speech. This understanding lies at the centre of Augustine's thought and prompts him to establish the grammar of theology itself: "more truly is God thought than said, and God is more truly than is thought".[39] It is from here all ontology flows, in recognition of a reality which

---

36 Already the way is marked by many false starts, such as Mark Taylor's attempts to appropriate the *via negativa* as a postmodern reality in Taylor, M. C., *Erring: A Postmodern A/theology*, Chicago, Chicago University Press, 1984.

37 Gregory of Nazianzus, *Theological Orations*, 2 esp. § 9. Text published in Norris F. W., *Gregory of Nazianzus, Faith Gives Fullness to Reasoning: the Five Theological Orations of Gregory Nazianzen*; translated by Wickham L. and Williams F., Leiden, E. J. Brill, 1991; for text see *Orationes: Discours de Grégoire de Nazianze 1-3*, translated by Bernardi, J., Paris, Éditions du Cerf, 1978, p. 182.

38 Gregory of Nyssa, *Commentary on the Song of Songs* in Jæger, W. (ed.), Gregorii Nysseni Opera; *Auxilio Aliorum Virorum Doctorum Edenda*, Vol. VI, Langerbeck, H. (ed.), *Gregorii Nysseni in Canticum Canticorum Edidit Hermannus Langerbeck*, Leiden, E. J. Brill, 1960.

39 "Verius enim cogitatur Deus quam dicitur, et verius est quam cogitatur." Augustine, *de Trinitate* Book VII, Ch. 4. It is this principle which Anselm was to develop in what was later termed the 'ontological argument' (Cf. Anselm, *Proslogion*, especially Book II).

cannot fit into any metaphysical system. It follows that if theological discourse is to speak truly, then it must be acutely attentive to itself and its limitations – it must be a language that operates with a grammar that simultaneously subverts it. This is theology's freedom, and the critique that it brings when engaging with all other systems of knowledge.

If theology cannot make of God an object, then theological discourse must speak in order to disclose presence. Indeed, it is the very disclosure of presence that opens up and sustains the possibility of this peculiar speech at all. In this way theology becomes not just a speech act, but worship. Theology therefore comes to its fullest expression in the liturgy and in community.[40] If theology simply remains within the academy, it falls under the illusion of its own competence and power; it becomes a language in the presence of self, not of Other. From a Catholic perspective the conversation begins, is nourished by, and attested in, community. The theological voice is never a personal voice, but always the voice of community; the speech in which the graced community hears and knows the faith it lives. This is why there can be magisterial voices, doctors of faith.

The Church is the locus and mediation of presence and knowledge, and as the community of discourse, it has epistemic and ontological depth; it is the most effective resistance to nihilism. If Radical Orthodoxy is to develop, it must also develop an ecclesiology, for without it theology relies too much on personality; it becomes a deracinated and alienated activity, prey to every fad that offers relevance and recognition. If it is to develop an ecclesiology, then finally Radical Orthodoxy must develop ecclesially: it must fulfil itself as Churched. No more than any of us, can it duck the question most posed in a nihilistic age, that of authority.

An ecclesiology also brings attention to the question of tradition that lies at the heart of hermeneutics.[41] In some sense, tradition must be the way in

---

40  This is well captured by Aquinas, *In Librum Boëthii de Trinitate*, I, Q. 2. a. 1. ad 6. "...quod deus honoratur silentio, non quod nihil de ipso dicatur vel inquiratur, sed quia quidquid de ipso dicamus vel inquiramus, intelligimus nos eius comprehensione defecisse, unde dicitur Eccli. 43 [32]: 'Glorificantes dominium quantumcumque potueritis, supervalebit adhuc'".

41  Cf. Blondel's seminal essay on *Tradition* in *The Letter on Apologetcs; and, History and Dogma*, London, Harvill, 1964, translated by Dru, A., and Trethowan, I. Blondel's notion of tradition is profoundly Christological, understanding it as part of the redemptive

which communities live in history and exercise freedom to discern the truth, and through these acts give form to their faith. Tradition is the way in which the ontology of faith comes to act, 'takes flesh' to witness to the unsurpassable reality of God in the act of his redemptive self-gift. It is the continuous discourse which keeps this act at its centre, in the knowledge that it can never be exhausted by our speaking. Its unity lies in its subject, the *mysterium salutis*, which can be nothing less than God himself.

Tradition is, therefore, one discourse in many voices; the record of the way in which that discourse and its form must change to be faith-full speech and witness. In this way tradition grounds each text and preserves the uniqueness of each voice. It does not relativise, because it understands the relationship of a period to what has gone before and will come after, hence it consciously gives each its own proper value. From this point of view, tradition arises out of the reality that it seeks to mediate: the sense that the *mysterium salutis* is universally present in history. Once more, it is Augustine who grounds a Catholic vision in the fact that all are moved sometimes by a universally present Truth.[42] In this he reaches far beyond the boundaries of a Platonic ontology to the God who is beyond being.

Tradition is also part of a redemptive movement, a healing of time, where the voices of history are not dead, but part of the living discourse of faith. If history is the realm of our fall, the experience of our not knowing, then it is precisely in, and through, history that we come to be redeemed by the presence of Christ. Tradition becomes the way in which the community rejects nihilism, because the very presence of Christ means that there never can be a nothingness in history. Tradition equally resists Nietzsche's 'will to power', for our freedom never was and never can be absolute; God in Christ

---

unfolding of Christ's self-offering and the Church's response: "Et voici le sens profond et décisif de la Tradition: la divine Victime est définie en son œuvre totale et en son *consummatum est: ipse tradidit semetipsum*" (*La Philosophie et L'Esprit Chrétien*, Vol. 11, Paris, Presses Universitaires de France, 1946, p. 79).

42  Augustine, *de Trinitate*, Book 14, Ch. 15. "...sed etiam ipse splendore aliquotiens ubique praesentis veritatis attingur quando admonitus confiteur." This is part of a general argument that even a person who does not know God and his Truth nevertheless has some sense of it when he recognises that he has done wrong, because the mind can know truth even if it does not know the one who is Truth. In such a way, to be human is to participate in God who is the eternal, hence everywhere present, Truth. Cf. Colossians 10[24].

has placed himself as the measure of meaning. Once we grasp this, then through that very relation, history becomes the sphere of a redeemed freedom, not a paradigm but a process through which we become meaning-full in and through our choices. Through tradition history is disclosed as a moral act, the field of our freedom before, and in, and through, God; not the practice of *scientia* but *sapientia*. It lives out of the understanding rightly articulated by Radical Orthodoxy: "All that there is, is only because it is more than it is".[43]

Our conversation continues because it is about God, God who is *semper maior*: not something arrived at through a logic of transcendence, but arrived at through the act of God's self-gift in the Son and in the Spirit. This is inexhaustible for every period, and history is our constant surprise encounter with this gift. It is this discovery that makes theology always, first and last, a word of gratitude. It is for this reason that 'no child of God needs to get back to the garden'. What could be more radical or orthodox?

43 *Radical Orthodoxy*, p. 4.

# Index